My Almost for His Highest

My Almost for His Highest

John Barber

WIPF & STOCK · Eugene, Oregon

MY ALMOST FOR HIS HIGHEST

Wipf and Stock
An Imprint of Wipf and Stock Publishers
199 W. 8th Ave., Suite 3
Eugene, OR 97401
www.wipfandstock.com

ISBN 13: 978-1-60899-632-2

Manufactured in the U.S.A.

Scripture quotations taken from the *New American Standard Bible*® unless otherwise noted, Copyright © 1960, 1962, 1963, 1968, 1971, 1972, 1973, 1975, 1977, 1995 by The Lockman Foundation. Used by permission.

Scripture quotations marked (KJV) are taken from the King James Version of the Bible.

To Paul, an insightful boy

Contents

Foreword

AFTER RETURNING HOME FROM the store on one occasion, my wife noticed on the receipt that she had not been charged for a 50-cent item. She immediately drove back to the store and paid for it. While a godless world may laugh at what they perceive as pettiness, we know that culpability has nothing to do with the price tag. The smallest compromise for the Christian is like a small leak in a large ship. In time, it matters.

There has been a serious leak within Christendom for the last hundred or so years. It began when the moral Law was forsaken as a schoolmaster to bring sinners to Christ. The effect was a loss of the fear of God. In time, themes such as repentance, Hell, sin, Judgment Day, the cross, justification, righteousness, holiness, and the exclusivity of Jesus Christ were discarded, sinking Christianity to an all-time low.

The devil promised the world to compromising preachers, and ironically, the father of lies kept his word. John Barber puts it this way, "The promised 'silver bullet' of success, which so many of us locked and loaded into our ministries, turned out to be a bullet in the brain. The multiplicity of exotic, seeker-sensitive methods, and other approaches as well—which we were assured would produce kingdom-results—have only pointed our ministries away from the target of God's Word and have now made us the target of God's hot displeasure."

If you want an ear-tickling book, then don't read this one. But if you have watched in horror as contemporary preachers turned their backs on Jesus because of His hard sayings, you will *love* this book. If you have refused to compromise with this world because you know that He alone has the words of eternal life, you will whisper "Amen" as you turn every uncompromising and truth-filled page.

Ray Comfort

Acknowledgments

THE TYPICAL ACKNOWLEDGMENTS PAGE lists those persons who made the book possible. Certainly this book is no different. You would not be holding this work in your hands right now were it not for the exceptional editorial skills of Ms. Tammy Campbell, long-time friend and Christian sister. I can also think of evangelist Ray Comfort whom I wish to thank for his willingness to place his name so close to mine in the writing of his fine foreword to this book. Then there is the publisher who was willing to put before the public what some may consider a "controversial book." Thanks to you. But most of all, I wish to thank God for always remaining faithful to his Word and to His Church, of which my family is a part. Where we would be without our faithful God? Thank you, dear Father.

Introduction

THERE ARE SEVERAL THINGS I would like you to know before you begin to read the main contents of this book.

First, in distinction from my academic works, this book is written in a simple style. To date, many books have been written on the theme of the decline of the evangelical churches and their witness. One of the things I've noticed, however, is that many people are not familiar with many of the words and concepts presented in some of these other fine books. In fact, I recall taking the time to literally rephrase sections of one of the most outstanding books on the topic for a friend so she could comprehend the gist of its main argument. It was then that the question entered my mind: "If so much of the problem within our evangelical community needs to be addressed among the laity, why are authors writing above their heads?" It was then that I decided that if ever I were to pen a similar book, I would try to keep the 50-cent words and phrases to a bare minimum. This book is not, therefore, written in a literary or sophisticated style. I have purposely kept it simple for people who wish to get to the point.

Second, this book is very hard hitting. What it lacks in prose it tries to make up for not only in clarity, but also in punch. I must admit that I have struggled a great deal with this aspect of the book. Most of the manuscript was completed in 2006, but then I sat on it for a very long time for the reason that, upon reflection, several sections of it seemed too terse, too dogmatic. My inability to resolve this issue held up the book's publication until now. Fundamentally, what concerned me is that we are all sinners. There is no perfect Christian, no perfect church or denomination. Because we all continue to struggle against indwelling sin, we walk with Christ on feet of clay. Consequently, we Christians are very easy targets. Why take aim at easy targets? What has one to prove? That he can hit an easy target?

Then, one day, as I was reading through portions of the Old Testament prophets, it was as if I felt afresh the heart of God for His people. The covenantal life of ancient Israel that Ezekiel and all of the other prophets address was broken almost beyond repair—idolatry, the worship of false gods, fornication, adultery, rank corruption at the highest levels of political, social, and religious life, lawlessness, and much more. Certainly the people under the old economy were easy targets. Yet God passionately and persistently sent common men to forcefully call His people back to obedience with warnings, strong and sure, of the consequences to come should they not turn back from their faithlessness. No less patiently God also held out the promises of blessedness should they return to Him, where there is life and joy in His presence.

For God, it's all black and white. No grays. Through holy men of old, God lovingly pursued His wayward children holding out clear options: life or death, light or darkness, heaven or hell, joy or bondage. "Easy targets?" Yes, I suspect we are. Perhaps that's all the more reason the message needs to be aimed at the bull's-eye with ultimate resolve.

Admittedly, this work is late entering the stream of literature on the subject. In contemplating why yet another book is needed, I was again reminded of the Old Testament prophets (not that I consider myself in their company, by any means)! My unspoken thought was, "Well, I guess Micah didn't say to himself, 'Isaiah and Jeremiah already dealt with all of this stuff. Why should I pick up the pen?'" I think that the long train of voices in our own day is again a sign of God's longsuffering with us, His love and graciousness and His desire not to judge us. He holds out the prospect of resolution without calamity for a very long time, using a number of different voices—all with their own individual temperament, tone, and key issues. But the day will finally come when He decides to wait no more and will withdraw the lampstand from many churches.

Third, this work deals in some depth with a number of individual issues. I have noticed that the literature on the subject paints many broad strokes regarding the dissolution of evangelical church life. What I find missing are extended comments dealing with actual areas within our communal life together. So, I have here attempted to marshal some thoughts on areas within our communities of faith that I believe are most lacking. I think that this procedure follows the outline of many of the prophets who show little hesitation when it comes to tackling individual practices. Whole chapters are thus set apart to deal with specific areas, some of which include corporate worship, preaching, Christian suffering, and church discipline. My list of issues is far from exhaustive but no less compelling.

Finally, I will state here what I will say again in the body of the work, though a little differently. There is much that is right with many of our churches. It is not my goal to deflate or denigrate an entire movement. Indeed, the Church of God is alive! As the Psalmist declares, "God is in the midst of her, she will not be moved" (Psalm 46:5). And Jesus promises "I will build My church; and the gates of Hades will not overpower it" (Matthew 16:18). What men may be doing in the name of Jesus for the purpose of ministry and church growth may run counter to God's intended design for His Body, and these patterns may be all but overtaking our contemporary evangelical church life, yet God has His remnant. God is still on the throne and His committed disciples are still here doing the work of spreading and establishing the kingdom of God on earth according to the Bible and in the power of the Holy Spirit.

Right now, the evangelical church is a remnant church. God knows the people and the churches that stand on His Word and those that do not. Though the overall spiritual condition of the evangelical movement is dire, fear not. God is again mustering an army. They're already at work; in fact, they never left their posts. This book is meant to encourage those prayer warriors who sit daily before God, crying out to Him for personal and corporate reformation, to "stand firm"—watching and waiting for the awakening power of our Lord to revive His people and nations. It's coming.

The following words are also intended to challenge those who have departed from the ways of God. If history teaches us anything, it's that there comes a point where the people's hearts are so deadened to the life of God, their ears so dull, and their appetites so set on having what the world has, that regardless of what is said, or how Spirit-filled the preacher is, they refuse to make an about face. It then rests with God to do with us as He wills. Let us heed the voice of the living God; let us return to Him, before He lovingly chastens us.

John Barber, PhD
2010

"Dad, We Need a Disco Ball!"

*"Character is always lost when a high ideal is sacrificed
on the altar of conformity and popularity."*

—CHARLES SPURGEON

EVANGELICALISM IS DYING. THE glory of God is ready to depart. As a movement, we're growing more and more content in the world. Rather than preferring to be absent from the body and present with the Lord, far too many of us prefer to be present with the body and with our future plans. We attend church. But mainly our interest is to learn how to improve our own lots in life. We're repeating the error of the impenitent thief on the cross to whom Jesus was only a matter of convenience. You can hear it in our prayers. Entreaties and petitions that once reflected verses of the Bible are now strangely at odds with Holy writ. The way He taught us to pray, with hearts submitted to his Kingdom rule, are more and more becoming images of modern man and his quest for successful living.

What has become of the spirit of brokenness and humility in our churches? We are forgetting to bow the knee. What has happened to the cry of the penitent thief who, in unassuming contrition, cried from the depths of his sin-sick soul, "Jesus, remember me when You come in Your kingdom!" We are forgetting we are thieves. Daily repentance and walking in true faith and holiness before God are being pushed aside to make room for the idols of personal relevance and the settled life.

What has become of our commitment to the crucified life? Have we forgotten His promise that we'll be persecuted for the sake of righteousness? To scores of Protestant believers the cross is a symbol, but that is all. What was once our joy to bear His cross turned to apprehension of it, and in our apprehension of it, we soon came to revile the very thought of losing face for His gospel. We are losing our saltiness.

Once there was a highway to heaven, full of born again souls set on pilgrimage to their heavenly Zion, a place not of this world. But now the highway is quickly being paved over with the veneer of casual Christianity. Other than the remaining trappings of ecclesiastical tradition found in some of our churches, or the name of Jesus heard through the loud speakers of culturally-sensitive extravaganzas called worship services found in others, very little evidence remains in the evangelical movement of what might be coined "evangelical."

A once powerful advance of bold, gospel proclamation, of men and women pouring out their hearts and souls in prayer to God, of a willingness to be a peculiar people amidst a world that knows not God, retains but the shell of its former self.

What is the cause of our sickness? *Evangelical leaders, and their followers, are relinquishing their commitment to the fundamentals of the Bible in order to induce church growth, regardless of the cost to the purity of the Church.* As a result, though many of our churches look prosperous on the outside, they are dying on the inside. What's so very sad is how few know it, and if they do know it, are unwillingly to admit it.

WHO AM I TALKING ABOUT?

I've used the term "evangelicalism." Many people think of evangelicalism and Christianity as one and the same. So perhaps the reader is wondering if I'm saying that Christianity is dying. Let me be clear regarding what I mean by the term evangelicalism and what it is that I object to.

Evangelicalism and Christianity are *not* identical. So please don't think that I take issue with Christianity or with the teachings of the Bible. Modern, Protestant evangelicalism is the offspring of early fundamentalism, itself birthed in the 1920s.[1] Fundamentalism was a movement of men and woman who opposed the modernism sweeping the culture and the leading seminaries and divinity schools of the early twentieth century. They committed themselves to "doing battle royal for the fundamentals" of the Bible. And what a movement it was. The basic presup-

---

1. My interest here is neither British Evangelicalism, birthed in Great Britain in the 1730s, nor the anti-intellectualism of the evangelical movement from 1925 to 1945. For a discussion of this latter idea, see Mark A. Noll, *The Scandal of the Evangelical Mind* (Grand Rapids: Eerdmans, 1994).

position that provided it with cohesion was the Bible's presentation of the supremacy of Christ over the whole of life.

Staunch loyalty to God-centeredness in all things enabled early twentieth-century reformers, such as B. B. Warfield, to call upon every particle of the creation to acknowledge its God. This same commitment made it possible for biblical scholars, most notably, J. Gresham Machen, to interpret liberal Christianity for what it really is: an oxymoron. Steadfastness before the fundamentals of the historic faith helped people interpret all man-centered forms of Christianity as struggling to keep pace with the Bible's presentation of the preeminence of Christ over His creation.

As the offspring of fundamentalism, evangelicalism maintained these basic commitments, but it wasn't long before key evangelical leaders began to develop their own sense of theological identity which produced some differences with the fundamentalist movement. Despite its alterations, for many years evangelicalism remained a biblical movement in radical opposition to theological liberalism.

Differently too, these evangelicals were dissimilar from other true believers, who kept the fundamentalist label but thought it best to remain "separate" from the world, a pietistic view. This split has remained intact to this day, with most evangelicals showing some commitment to the Cultural Mandate of Scripture to engage with the world, and a good number of fundamentalists adopting an "other-world" stance toward culture. Next to theological liberals and pietistic fundamentalists, evangelicalism can therefore be described as the "third leg" of American Protestantism.

The Big Downward Slide

Beginning in the early 1970s, truly negative modifications occurred within the evangelical movement. These modifications came mainly from two sources: 1) the inclusion of business, psychological, and social theories in the related areas of church growth, evangelism, and missions; and 2) a softening position *in general* toward the role of the Bible in church life and doctrine. What opened the door to these trends was an even more basic problem, which I've already mentioned: a willingness within our churches and theological schools to generate church expansion regardless of the price to the integrity of the Church.

It's this ungodly attitude, and the trends it's invited into an ever-increasing number of our churches, that I object to—some of which I've already alluded to but will have much more to say about in the following sections.

Worship Wars?

To further clarify my objections, let me say that I don't protest contemporary worship services. An evangelical church can have a very biblically-oriented, contemporary worship style with the content of the service focused on biblical ideas, usually coinciding with the sermon topic. The church's small group discipleship model is also Christ-centered, designed to help believers mature so they can reach others for Christ, who will in turn mature, and so on. It's the multiplication model. So I want to place a distinction between a church that might have a contemporary style, but has all of the fundamentals in place, and a church which is all style and no substance. It's this latter group, which is evolving and providing a prophetic indicator of the future shape of the evangelical movement, to which I object most strenuously.

The Inward-looking Congregation

There is a separate group of churches I'm also greatly concerned about, but of which I'll have a bit less to say in the coming chapters. These are the evangelical churches which are quite traditional in worship and have remained committed to biblical doctrine and method, but they've earned a place on my list of worst offenders because they bear the mark of "Laodicea." They're not giving their utmost for His highest, but are "lukewarm." In these fortresses of truth, there is no joy, no sense of expectation in worship, no burden for the lost, and no intention of reaching the "outcast" for Christ. They're just going through the motions. They must learn, as Luther penned, it's not a mighty fortress is our church, but our God!

AN INSIGHTFUL BOY

I've thought about the declining state of Protestant, evangelical Christianity for years. First, I think, as a result of my own personal failures as a believer. The ways in which this writer has failed to measure up to the standard of the gospel could fill a memoir a thousand pages long!

The higher calling of Christianity is something to which I continuously strive, and which incessantly beckons me to elevate my walk with Him, to be more like Jesus. In addition to my own shortcomings, what else has motivated me to think on the subject at hand is, as I've stated, the waning, spiritual condition of an alarming number of our churches.

One day the problem manifested in my heart with uncommon clarity. It was a typical, hot and humid summer day in South Florida when I was driving my teenage son, Paul, home from his drum lesson. At some point, I blurted out to him, "You know our church really needs to grow." Throughout the day I had been thinking about our church and of its need to further develop thriving, God-centered ministry, not only within our body, but also to the surrounding community.

My comment was followed by a brief few seconds of dull silence when suddenly Paul gleefully responded, "Dad, we need a disco ball! You know, like the one I saw when I visited that giant church."

Paul was recounting a time when we lived in Central Florida, and one of his friends had invited him to attend church with his family. The "disco ball" comment jogged my memory of that weekend and especially of my son's description to his mother and me of the church's worship service. I'll never forget what he said. After mentioning what appeared to him as a disco ball hanging from the ceiling,[2] he went on and on about how little mention had been made during the service about the important truths of Jesus' person and work for our sins. He concluded that the whole time was nothing more than "an experience in pop culture."

This was coming from a young boy with absolutely no formal training in how to plan and lead a Christian worship service. I must say that I was proud of my son and his keen discernment.

Popularizing the Church

Though Paul was only joking that the secret to this one church's success lay in its disco ball, and that our church could repeat its achievement by getting one of our own, the sad fact is that the disco ball might very well stand as a symbol for an increasingly dangerous move in today's church—the watering down of biblical ministry in order to garnish success.

---

2. The church Paul visited was meeting in a renovated roller-rink, and the large ball-shaped lights in the ceiling were never removed.

There is nothing wrong with big churches. Indeed, numerical growth is something God expects of His Church. Back in the pages of the Old Testament, God promises Abram and his wife, Sarah, that their "seed"—a prophetic reference to Jesus Christ of Nazareth—will produce as many spiritual descendents as there are grains of sand along the seashore and stars lining the night sky. Apply this truth to ministry and you can see that exponential, numerical growth is something God promises His Church and which He also expects.

So, church growth is not the problem. The problem is our mounting desertion of the Bible to attain that growth. Our dying condition is the result of a self-inflicted wound. The promised "silver bullet" of success, which so many of us locked and loaded into our ministries, turned out to be a bullet in the brain. The multiplicity of exotic, seeker-sensitive methods, and other approaches as well—which we were assured would produce kingdom-results—have only pointed our ministries away from the target of God's Word and have now made us the target of God's hot displeasure.

Permit me to make some general observations on the larger *cultural context* which is precipitating the far-reaching replacement of biblically-based ministry with other means that many churches are now using to cultivate progress.

MINISTRY IN A POST-CHRISTIAN AGE

To the credit of visionary leaders who have challenged the Church to help fulfill the Great Commission in our day, the gospel message is reaching areas of the world previously unimagined even fifty years ago. With this evangelistic task has come a need to address an insidious ideology that many claim calls upon us to rethink our tried and true approaches in ministry. It is called postmodernism.

Postmodernism is still a relatively new area in the study of secular philosophy that looks to complex theories of language as a way to interpret life according to social rather than individual categories. In our day, postmodern thought has affected many areas of human culture, from art and architecture to politics. It has also touched theology. Essentially, the theory assumes that people are entirely the product of their cultural and social surroundings. "Truth" is therefore what is true for each culture. Moral choice, so the theory holds, isn't the responsibility of the individual, but is the product of cultural and social pressures that are beyond his control.

According to postmodern thought, then, there is no objective reality, no absolute truth. People are only cogs in a wheel who only imagine they are making free moral choices. A young inner-city male, for example, robs a convenience store, not because he's a bad person, but because his upbringing *made* him that way. We would therefore be wrong to expect people to think or to act differently than how their environment has shaped them. Problematically, it's impossible to hold anyone answerable for their behavior under this account of right verses wrong.

"Can You Hear Me Now?"

Coupled with the idea that people are products of their surrounding culture is the notion that *language* is also a prisoner of culture. According to postmodern thought, each culture has its own value system that can *only* be understood through the medium of language appropriate to that culture. The very notion of *revealed truth*, therefore, is not something postmodern people are attracted to; in fact, they will likely consider the proposition pompous and conceited. They may even go as far as to characterize the suggestion that there is a universal language that can critique all people's worldview and behavior as disdainful of others' cultural identity, something which can easily lead to elitism and racism.

So, if a postmodern person does look for a church to attend, it will certainly not be one where moral absolutes are taught and modeled. He is more concerned with the *experience* of church, not its doctrine.

CHURCHES AT THE CROSSROADS

Facing the challenge of postmodernism is the minister of the gospel. The choice before him has been made simple. Either stick to the power of the gospel to change lives or allow the culture to dictate the rules of engagement. Unfortunately, more and more church leaders are choosing the latter course of action. The choice has been made easy for those willing to barter away their commitment to the essentials of the Bible for the potential of church growth. These church leaders, backed by their followers, now openly confess that people's real problem is not their sin nature. It's that the environment has *caused* them to reject religious truth.

Following the postmodern notion that *language* is also a prisoner of culture, fewer preachers are willing to use words such as "born-again," "repentance," and "atonement" in their sermons out of their belief that these words are culturally-conditioned and therefore present a stumbling block to effective communication with contemporary people. They're reticent to declare that someday God will separate "the sheep from the goats" and "the wheat from the chaff" because they're certain that the average person no longer identifies with such archaic concepts. If any of this sounds familiar, it should. Its postmodern thought redressed in ecclesiastical garb.

In the postmodern church, ministry is to be crafted along the lines of what the unregenerate mind is willing to absorb. So seeker services are replacing worship services, divine encounters are being encouraged in place of the born again experience, pep-talks are being substituted for the exposition of the Bible, therapy is replacing biblical counseling, entertainment is taking the place of evangelism, and the fear of man is trumping the fear of God.

These churches provide no absolutes, no final word, no line in the sand, and no "thus sayeth the Lord." Their unspoken motto is "no confrontation." Pastors who lead these churches elude the "shalts" and "shalt nots" of Scripture with a skill reminiscent of master sailors circumventing the isles of Rhode Island's Narragansett Bay. In all, the evangelical movement is gradually relinquishing its role as guardian of God's truth and is becoming a mere facilitator of the seeker, whose interest in spiritual things is limited to limply exploring the meaning and relevance of the Christian experience for his felt needs. We are witnessing a redefining of biblical Christianity right in front of our noses.

An Ironic Twist

The unintended consequence of accommodating Christianity to the caprice of the culture is that those who are responsible for the act have adopted secular thinking as their own. This only points to a profound fact. *Every time the Church permits the culture to construct the framework for the discussion about the nature and reality of truth it becomes the very thing it hates.* Unfortunately, no church leader, or congregant, who has caved to the culture, will admit what they've become. But it's true, nonetheless. The spiritual condition of our Protestant communities is rapidly approaching that of the people of ancient Judah, to whom God declared through the mouth of the prophet, "How the faithful city has become a harlot, she who was full of justice! Righteousness once lodged in her, but now murderers. Your silver has become dross, your drink diluted with water" (Isaiah 1:21–22).

HOPE FOR THE FUTURE

I hope I've been clear that for me to say that the evangelical movement is "dying," shouldn't be taken to suggest that the Church of God is dying. Nor does it suggest that faithfulness to the truths of the Scriptures has been entirely lost within the evangelical movement. A love for the truth of God's Word can be found in many of our large churches, and also in little out-of-the-way churches, where pastors labor in the basement of obscurity. This love is also still detected in the teachings of many missionaries abroad, and in homes where children are treated to loving parents who talk of how a Jesus who is not Lord of all, is not Lord at all. But as a whole, the Lordship of Christ, and its attendant doctrines and practices, are no longer central to the evangelical cause.

Nonetheless, there is hope. The remnant can rebuild the ancient walls. Together we can foster a new future of revival and reformation. But like Warfield, Machen, and their contemporaries, and like the magisterial Reformers of old, we dare not rely on the dried stump of dead, man-centered religion to rebuild the ruins. We must nurture biblical Christianity where others have abandoned it in pursuit of celebrity and large congregations at any cost. We will not get our pictures on the cover of a famous Christian magazine, but at least we can look ourselves in the mirror.

Next, I will flesh out a good bit of what has been addressed in this chapter by interacting with three fundamental assumptions people use to support the new philosophy of ministry.

2

Pulling Back the Screen on the Wizard of Evangelicalism

"If there are certain principles, as I think there are, which the constitution of our nature leads us to believe, and which we are under a necessity to take for granted in the common concerns of life, without being able to give a reason for them; these are what we call the principles of common sense; and what is manifestly contrary to them is what we call absurd."

—THOMAS REID

"PAY NO ATTENTION TO the man behind the curtain," bemoans the Wizard of Oz, as his fantasy world is exposed. Caught in the hypocrisy of his own creation, the mechanisms of his illusions are revealed as gimmicks. Many churches are not much different than the Wizard. No longer relying on the all-sufficiency of Scripture, Christ crucified and raised, holiness of life, and the ministry of the Holy Spirit to spread and to establish the Church, they've turned to all the latest tricks, techniques, and programs which are said to promise large congregations. Churches with deep pockets even go as far as to use attention-grabbing, theatrical productions to draw throngs of people. But just like in the Wizard of Oz, it's all an illusion.

It's time we pull back the screen and reveal the wizard for what he is. Let's do so by exposing the three basic assumptions churches use to justify their desertion of biblical ministry for new, popularized approaches calculated to appeal to man's lower nature. They are that 1) the traditional way of doing church is out of touch with un-churched people; 2) un-churched people increasingly do not understand the language of the Church; 3) un-churched people are reluctant to come to church because they find it difficult to identify with Christians.

THE TRADITIONAL WAY OF DOING CHURCH IS OUT OF TOUCH WITH UN-CHURCHED PEOPLE

The word "un-churched" is relatively new in evangelical parlance. The word is to the church growth movement what the phrase "undocument-ed worker" is to the immigration debate. The word is intended to soften the harsh offense of man's total depravity and to recast the discussion on ministry and evangelism in a new light. The point of which is to say that the un-churched are not alienated to the gospel by nature, but are merely postmodern people whose spiritual condition is due to strong social and cultural influences that are not within their control.

Maybe they weren't raised in a Christian home or didn't attend Sunday school to hear Bible stories. Or perhaps due to the increasing secularization of society, they weren't exposed to Christian cultural values while growing up. So then, the real problem with the un-churched, so the suggestion goes, is not that they are sinners—they are just uninformed.[1] Many shepherds now feel it's their job to somehow reverse this trend. The process begins with providing a warm and inviting church experience that will encourage the reeducation process to take shape so that over time the un-churched person will embrace a new set of assumptions revolving around the gospel and become a Christian.

An Assessment

What are we to make of this approach? Let's start by clearing the air. Apart from the obvious idea that every church ought to provide a warm and inviting environment for worship, people who are not Christians are *not* merely un-churched. They're *lost*. Their sin has incurred the very judgment of a holy and all-wise God. The Bible records, "He who believes in Him is not judged; he who does not believe has been judged already, because he has not believed in the name of the only begotten Son of God" (John 3:18).

Nonetheless, it's not uncommon to meet someone who claims to be unfamiliar with some of the more fundamental assumptions about life

---

1. As I stated in the previous chapter, this position is itself influenced by postmodern thought.

that Christians take for granted. Western culture is not the repository of values it once was. However, we must not forget the biblical truth that regardless of a society's morality, or lack thereof, people always possess some knowledge of objective truth. Whether it is the image of God in man, or the way nature points to the handiwork of the Creator, natural revelation serves as an inescapable testimony of the existence of God and of the judgment to come. In his speech at Mars Hill, Paul linked the design found in the world to the fact that there is a designer. He was confident that he was appealing to an innate knowledge of God deeply hidden inside the hearts of the Greek philosophers to whom he spoke (Acts 17:26–27).

It's also highly inaccurate to say that non-Christians are products of their surrounding culture. Fundamentally, people aren't products of culture. They're products of Adam. Paul writes, "Therefore, just as through one man sin entered into the world, and death through sin, and so death spread to all men, because all sinned" (Romans 5:12). While it is true that people are largely *influenced* by culture and their cultural preferences can, and often do, change from one shift in culture to the next, we must never forget that the lost are poisoned from head to toe by the effects of original sin.

Spiritually speaking, sinners are graveyard dead. This means that the church that tailors its corporate worship *strictly* along the lines of the cultural preferences of sinners is the church that tunes its piano to the slamming of a coffin lid.

Is the Church Out of Touch?

The wide-ranging acceptance of market-driven outreach has come with an indictment of churches that have remained committed to historic, Protestant practices in communal worship. The charge is that they're "out of touch." Critics say that most people simply don't want to come to a church where a plate is passed under their noses and the music is from a by-gone age. Out-of-date liturgical practices and the use of theological vocabulary, so we are told, have further created an inhospitable climate leaving un-churched people out in the cold. The charge is ratcheted up with the insistence that many churches have literally "disenfranchised" unbelievers. That's a heavy charge. To disenfranchise means to "banish or to excommunicate." If unbelievers have done nothing to earn their banishment, then the traditional church has maliciously exiled an entire generation of unreached people. Is this true?

The picture of rejected people turned away from fellowship with God by stuck-in-the-mud, traditionalist churches, turns the Bible on its head. The Scriptures teach that all people are to honor the Sabbath and worship God on that day, regardless of what type of worship service is offered to them (Exodus 20:8, Hebrews 10:25). No doubt many churches are not prepared to relate to the various subcultures potentially represented in their services on any given Sunday. But this is a practical concern that has more to do with addressing people's preferences. God does not expect churches to make unbelievers' preferences a major principle of biblical worship.

The Great Seduction

Innovative church planners are correct about one thing. Most non-Christians are resistant to the idea of "church." However, if we look at the unbeliever's resistance to the Church from a biblical point of view, it becomes clear that what he's really bucking isn't offering plates and dry organ music. Rather, the "old man"—the sinful nature—is resistant to the idea of conforming to Christ. Paul writes to Timothy, "[P]reach the word; be ready in season and out of season; reprove, rebuke, exhort, with great patience and instruction. For the time will come when they will not endure sound doctrine; but wanting to have their ears tickled, they will accumulate for themselves teachers in accordance to their own desires, and will turn away from the truth and will turn aside to myths" (2 Timothy 4:2–4). Why does Paul write these words? Because people want to hear good words, pleasing words, comforting words.

People say, "Oh I would go to church if they just wouldn't beg for money. I'd gladly join if the minister didn't sound so preachy." So, what have many churches done? They've tailored their worship services to what the unregenerate mind is willing to absorb. Like a man courting a young lady, they drop those added pounds brought on by too much doctrine. They eliminate the offering basket and the tithe because that would be like asking your date to pay for her meal. And many don't even mention the word "sin" from the pulpit because that would be equivalent to telling your date she's ugly.

But it's all a seduction. The church that courts unbelievers rather than minister to them always ends up with less gospel, fewer standards, and a smaller distinction between it and the world it claims to be reaching. The sinner can't possibly know his spiritual needs because his heart is darkened by sin. He thus lacks the objectivity required to judge his spiritual needs. Paul writes, "But a natural man does not accept the things of the Spirit of God, for they are foolishness to him; and he cannot understand them, because they are spiritually appraised" (1 Corinthians 2:14). The unbeliever doesn't know if he needs fewer hymns, longer sermons, or no sermon. All he knows is that he does *not* want the God of the Bible.

We Need the Power of God

Clearly there are legitimate questions churches must ask that pertain to the contextualization of the gospel in a modern world, such as, "How is the gospel received by people of different subcultures?" The fact is that I write music for contemporary worship teams. In fact, I choose to embrace both the old and the new in worship. In my incorporation of the old and the new has come many hours of thinking hard about effective ways to embrace unbelievers in public worship without compromising God's will and ways on the Sabbath. Presently, an increasing number of evangelical churches place far too much emphasis on contextualization and not enough upon the power of the gospel to minister to people of different subcultures. As important as contextualization is, the power of God in ministry is that much more important.

Isn't it interesting that if we were to follow the advice of many mission boards which are consumed with matching missionaries with their best "ministry fit," we would send Paul, the Jew, to minister to the Jews, and Peter, the Gentile, to minister to the Gentiles. But Jesus reversed the order, sending Paul to the Gentiles, and Peter to the Jews. Why? In part, to demonstrate that the spreading of the Kingdom of God doesn't depend on the contextualization of the gospel, but on the power of God's Word and Spirit. The gospel is indeed the "power of God for salvation to everyone who believes" (Romans 1:16).

UN-CHURCHED PEOPLE INCREASINGLY DO NOT UNDERSTAND THE LANGUAGE OF THE CHURCH

As mentioned before, many evangelical church leaders avoid biblical words and phrases in their communication with unbelievers. This abandonment is based in the erroneous, postmodern notion that talking to a contemporary person about the Bible is a cross-cultural experience. People, so we are told, no longer understand the culturally-bound language of the Bible. But the Bible is not culturally-bound language. It's the Word of God!

The historic Christian faith has always asserted that *all* Scripture, including words like "born-again," "Savior," and "redemption," is the inerrant, infallible, authoritative Word of God. Each word of Scripture is "God-breathed." When unbelievers come into contact with the Word of God, either through hearing or reading, a supernatural force, not culturally-bound language, confronts them.

The modern view of Scripture touted by contemporary evangelicals echoes a very dangerous position heralded by the late Swiss theologian Karl Barth (1886–1968), the father of neo-orthodoxy. He argued in his commentary on the *Epistle to the Romans,* and in other of his writings, that the Bible "becomes" the Word of God to those whom God reveals it. In other words, though Barth calls the Bible "God's Word," he isn't willing to say that the Bible *is* the Word of God. Rather, God's Word is nothing else than the free disposing of God's grace. For Barth, then, God's Word is identical to the ministry of the grace of God to unbelievers. The Bible simply facilitates the experience.

The danger of Barth's position is that the words of Scripture become dispensable. They are merely a means to an end. Building upon Barth's views, liberal Protestantism, seen predominantly in the old, mainline churches, argues that if at a future date changes in culture necessitate the use of different words that better point to God's grace, the Church should adopt them.

Barth's positions were denounced by orthodox scholars of his day, and yet, the spirit of his teachings has resurfaced in the Church through the evangelical emphasis on contextualization. It's now virtually impossible to attend a church planting seminar or an evangelism conference without hearing how many of the words of Scripture are dispensable because they no longer communicate to a postmodern audience. But the person who says that the words of Scripture no longer carry the same power they once had may as well be saying that God had a plan to communicate the gospel from the time of Christ to the early-twentieth century when suddenly He ran out of gas. Poor God. He didn't foresee postmodernism!

But the Bible contradicts this ridiculous notion. It says, "For the word of God is living and active and sharper than any two-edged sword, and piercing as far as the division of soul and spirit, of both joints and marrow, and able to judge the thoughts and intentions of the heart. And there is no creature hidden from His sight, but all things are open and laid bare to the eyes of Him with whom we have to do" (Hebrews 4:12–13).

The Dissolution of Absolute Truth

Many evangelicals further argue that it is vanity to try to present biblical truth to the average postmodern person because to do so is to appeal to a form of righteousness that no longer exists in the West. With the steep decline of values in America and in Europe has come an unleashing of destructive influences upon the family and society at large. The increased rates of broken families, crime, and sexual promiscuity have only added to the lessening sense of morality. The increasing denial of absolute truth in our day is said to make ministry in general, and evangelism in particular, more difficult.

The proposed solution is for the Church to rebuild the foundation of truth through "preevangelism." Preevangelism, which takes place in scores of evangelical worship services, seeks to expose people to the idea of absolutes slowly and in a non-confrontational manner, handling them with kid gloves all along the way, in the hope that they will not jump ship. The sermon must therefore emphasize God's love and grace over judgment. It's hoped that, after a period of time, the gentle approach will warm sinners to the notion of absolute truth whereby, at a later time, they can be approached with the Good News in which sin and salvation are unabashedly expressed.

Some Obvious Inconsistencies

There are two problems with this theory.

First, churches tend to remain stuck in the preevangelism mode and never get to the point of declaring the fullness of the gospel.

Second, the preevangelism theory is in error because it gives far too much credence to the role society's attitude toward absolute truth plays in the area of ministry. For example, the theory argues that people were more responsive to the gospel in puritan America because back then the Bible occupied a central place in society. All of this has changed, we are told, making ministry far more difficult and in need of serious renovation. But the proper context to evaluate evangelism's effectiveness in the hearts of unregenerate people is not sociology, but theology. Paul writes, "So then He has mercy on whom He desires, and He hardens whom He desires" (Romans 9:18). We can take from the apostle's point that the Spirit of God is sovereign in calling dead hearts to the glorious promise of the Good News regardless of where societies stand, from age to age, on the subject of absolute truth.

Moreover, we can argue that although fallen man is spiritually dead, he retains vestiges of the image of God and is surrounded by the testimony of nature to the existence of the Creator. In evangelism, it's this natural revelation the Holy Spirit appeals to through the ministry of the Word of God. Thus the man who denies the existence of absolute truth is a liar. And the man who says that an unbeliever must embrace a minimum level of social values before the gospel can work effectively in his life is biblically uninformed. That some may dismiss the gospel is again a matter reserved to the sovereignty of God and can't be blamed on a lack of nominally-accepted truths within society.

UN-CHURCHED PEOPLE ARE RELUCTANT TO COME TO CHURCH BECAUSE THEY FIND IT DIFFICULT TO IDENTIFY WITH CHRISTIANS

Some time ago, I had the opportunity to listen to a leading evangelical figure present a speech before a conference of lay-evangelists. He said, "If you were to ask the average person their opinion of Christians, they'd tell you they are angry people." He went on to detail the great mistakes conservative Christians have made by confronting the ills of society, such as homosexuality and abortion, arguing that our virulent stand has chased people away from the Church.

He furthered his discussion stating that, in order to attract people back to the fold, our calculated plan should be to change the world's bad perception of Christians. Once people understand that all that Christians want to do is to pray for them, bless them, and to help meet their needs, they'll see we're really nice people and the gospel will gain a hearing once again. It was extremely clear this gentleman was speaking the mind of many other prominent evangelical church leaders in attendance at the conference.

Progressively, evangelicals are of the mind that Christians who engage in a protracted battle with unrighteousness, whether in the Church, or in civil society, are missing the heart of God. The new approach to ministry, they say, should be marked by a tame and passive posture toward sin with the belief that mercy and grace will triumph. Mercy and grace are biblical. But remove the church's prophetic stand against sin and evil and what remains is a domesticated, liberalized church that places a higher premium on making friends with the world than on winning the world to God.

An Uncomfortable Truth

Jesus Christ would have rejected the argument that unbelievers' reticence toward the Gospel is based on their opinion of Christians. According to the Bible, people's estimation of Christians is irrelevant in evangelism. Jesus went as far as to say, "You will be *hated* by all because of My name" (Matthew 10:22, italics mine). In the Sermon on the Mount, Jesus told His disciples to be "poor in spirit," "gentle," and "merciful." Even then, He said, "people will insult you and persecute you, and falsely say all kinds of evil against you, because of Me" (Matthew 5:11). According to our Lord, not only will men hate us, but they will do so even when we're on our *best* behavior.

How then ought we to account for the unbeliever's hostility to the gospel? The Bible teaches that sinners are *by nature* at enmity with God (Romans 5:10). The world's hatred of believers is a reflection of its inbred hatred of Christ. Again, He said that we will be despised on account of His My name. (Matthew 10:22; see also John 15:18). The believer must always assume a biblical/theological reason for people's resistance to the Gospel—something only the Gospel can break through (Acts 8:14).

Was Jesus an Angry Christian?

If anything, Luke 10 could serve as a model for increased antagonism between Christians and unbelievers. Jesus said if a city rejects His disciples, they're to go into the city streets and say, "Even the dust of your city which clings to our feet, we wipe off in protest against you; yet be sure of this, that the kingdom of God has come near" (v.11). The disciples were as much charged with condemning the cities as they were with reaching them. But no one denounced the faithlessness of the cities more than Jesus, who said, "I say to you, it will be more tolerable in that day for Sodom, than for that city" (v.12). Sounds to me like Jesus must have been one of those angry Christians.

Having addressed the three chief justifications that faddish churches use to support their new ministry model, let's now turn our gaze to the strategic approach such churches use to achieve their defining goals: the need for *innovation* in Christian ministry.

3

How to Shatter the Crystal Cathedral
with the Primal Scream

"To innovate is not to reform."

—Edmund Burke

SOME YEARS AGO, MY wife and I were vacationing in California. While in the L.A. area, we decided to stop in and see the Crystal Cathedral. During our visit, I ran into a man who served on the church staff, and with whom I struck up a brief conversation. I really don't know what prompted my remark, but I coyly said, "You know, a lot of people don't think you guys are preaching the gospel. Do you really believe that positive thinking is the gospel?" A smile slowly spread across his face. Then he replied, "You don't understand. The message of positive thinking gets people in the door. Once they're here, we work at exposing them to the gospel through Bible studies and numerous other kinds of small group settings. Without the message of positive thinking, they'd never even show up."

I thanked the man for his comments and told him I'd think them over.

OUR ANNUAL RANKING OF AMERICA'S LARGEST CHURCHES. AND THE WINNERS ARE . . .

"How do we attract people to church?" is a relevant question. It's particularly perplexing among churches that are convinced that the culture has passed them by. Believing that people no longer see the local church as a great place to involve family and to discover friends, more and more congregations now look askance at the old tried-and-true methods that once made their church a place of interest to neighbors. Invite-a-friend Sunday, the yearly Christmas and Easter concerts, the annual Spring Revival, and VBS have all grown stale. What we need, so people pronounce, is *innovation* in ministry.

Don't forget that word—innovation. It crops up at every turn in the planning of the modern church. The word is a call for new, cutting edge approaches to ministry, calculated to magnetize people back to the fold. To meet this demand some larger churches go as far as to offer saunas, complete work-out facilities, computer arcade centers for kids, different musical formats for each Sunday of the month, dancers, internet feeds that link together churches hundreds of miles apart, eye-popping buildings, massive budgets, multi-media presentations, and much, much more.

A Vicious Cycle

While innovation is now being applied to a broad spectrum of ministries, its main focus is *the worship setting*. True, many Protestant worship services are overly provincial and could use a facelift. But overemphasis on innovation in worship bears an unintended consequence. It pours more worldly junk into people already full of worldly junk, especially the myriad of ways they find to entertain themselves.

Just consider the computer-based amusement center sitting in either your office, or in your kid's bedroom, which might include YouTube, Facebook, Skype, and Second Life. In order to draw people to church, ministry strategists now feel the necessity to compete with the world for people's up-to-the-minute cultural appetites. So they try to offer superior attractions, superior enticements, and superior glitter in the form of entertainment-driven worship services. The result of this unnecessary competition has left a multitude of evangelical church attendees suffering from *spiritual bulimia*: always consuming but never digesting. They can't digest the hyped up displays being passed off as worship services because they arrive to church already full of the things of the world.

Did you know that the French verb *bourrer*, which means "to stuff," is the source of the English word, boredom? What this tells us is that people are bored, not because they have too little with which to occupy themselves, but too much. Boredom is the state of being stuffed.

Paradoxically, boredom in Christian worship is the natural response to being entertained after already having gorged oneself on entertainment Monday through Saturday. People leaving modish, communal worship services may leave looking full. But deep down inside they're still spiritually hungry, a hunger which compels them back into the world to find a distraction, a movie, a computer game, perhaps a sport, to embellish their lives and gain a sense of fulfillment—fleeting though it may be. It's a vicious cycle.

Churches that try to draw people in using overblown, worldly incentives, only to leave them in a state of spiritual hunger, remind me of that piece of mail you get which says, "You've won a prize." Included are directions to where you can collect your free prize. But once you arrive, what do you discover? The whole thing is a time-share pitch in the Bahamas. They know you'd never come in response to the pitch, so the free prize is the lure. Turns out, the prize wasn't free after all. What's worse, you're still likely to leave empty-handed.

But this isn't ministry. The Church shouldn't try to compete with the world's consumer mentality in order to attract people to services. God doesn't expect His churches to be as action packed as the latest Bond movie, slick as a Madison Avenue ad campaign, or as convenient and multifunctional as the latest computer. Jesus promises so *much more*. He said, "I am the bread of life; he who comes to Me will not hunger, and he who believes in Me will never thirst" (John 6:35). This should be our goal for corporate worship: to minister true spiritual refreshment and nourishment—the "Bread of life."

Originality or Bust!

Perhaps no example better articulates the quest for innovation in ministry than the new attitudes toward church "vision statements." Churches that elevate innovation to a spiritual discipline automatically seek to craft vision statements in such a way as to underscore their uniqueness as compared with other churches. It needs to be this way, so we are informed, because what attracts people to a church is what is exceptional about it. Basically, then, such a vision statement will want to say to people, "You need to be here because we're different from all the others." None of this is based in Scripture, of course, but represents ideas borrowed from mainstream marketing which assumes that that which attracts people to a store is what sets it apart from all the others.

But join me in thinking back over the great confessions and creeds of church history, such as the Apostle's Creed and the Nicene Creed.

Though their principal intent was to clarify what the Bible teaches on key subjects so as to defend orthodoxy against the encroachment of pagan belief, local churches also embraced these documents as a means to let visitors know they weren't attending a schismatic group, but a church that is part of a worldwide network of Bible-believing churches, in short, a true, Christian church. Thus, the ancient, written statements—which individual churches embraced—didn't seek to emphasize a church's originality but its unanimity with other, true churches.

Conversely, overly sophisticated churches of today see little to no benefit in articulating their oneness with other churches. In reality, when it comes to the historic creeds and confessions of the Church their attitude tends to be wholly dismissive.

So what further observations can we make of innovative approaches designed to attract people to church?

PUTTING THE "NO" IN INNOVATION

The stark reality is that innovative churches have innovated themselves right out of the Bible. To use excessively ingratiating efforts to curry favor with sinners through some marketing thingamajig, a bit of bait, if you will, so they will check you out and be inclined to remain, is an affront to Christ. It's an affront to the biblical nature of the Church as well. *The average evangelical church has become an adult recreational center with sacraments.* The progressive church needs to come to grips with a simple fact. *Innovation is not a sign of the Church.*

In response, people caution that if our churches are to reach the children of the computer-age it must think "outside the box." But why are we thinking outside the box when the answers for modern man are still in the box? As a musician, I can't help but think of this analogy.

Classical and country represent different styles of music. They're different in inspiration but are similar insofar as both styles depend upon established music theory. In thinking outside the box, evangelical pacesetters have invented the equivalent of a new *ministry theory* God never gave His Church the authority to use. They remind me of the contemporary composer John Cage (1912–1992), known for his radical use of new sounds, phrases, and concepts in music.[1] Cage drew inspiration

---

1. Though John Cage has been heralded as the greatest influence in modern music, most of his creations compile a cacophony of sounds and a nonsensical use of musical instruments and recording equipment which fail to reflect God's beauty and His created order.

from religious patterns as diverse as Hindu aesthetics and the medieval Christian mystic Meister Eckhart to compose "far out," ultramodern music which he hoped would quiet the mind of listeners and make them susceptible to divine influences.

The new direction in ministry is like this: concentrated on making people amenable, suggestible, and disposed to Christian influences in which they will encounter the "Divine." But *God doesn't anticipate us investing our energy in experimental ministry that is ahead of its time. He expects us to minister the Word of God to the times in which we live.*

An Ancient Problem

The ploy to use bait to attract people to a particular church over another is not new. For centuries, Roman Catholic and Eastern Orthodox churches have boasted of relics of the saints (preserved objects connected with the great men and women of the past—a sword, a coat, a book) that the faithful could visit and venerate. Relics have been venerated since the earliest days of the Church. When St. Ignatius of Antioch was martyred in about 110 A.D., two of his companions came by night and gathered up his bones. In the same century, after Saint Polycarp was burned alive, Christians gathered his ashes for veneration. The earliest Christians errantly believed that although the bodies of the saints were, in life, temples of the Holy Spirit, they remained, in death, powerful instruments of God that deserved esteem. The church that had such relics attracted people who believed that close contact with relics brought blessings bestowed by God.

It was only natural, then, that abuses would arise regarding these so-called relics—namely a keen rivalry between churches over who owned the superior relic. The church with a relic of the veil of the Virgin Mary, for example, could count on attracting more people than the church that exhibited a relic from St. Barnabas. One band of ancient monks even went as far as to steal the body parts of certain martyrs and bring them to their church hoping to gain more converts.

Though there have been numerous claimants to relics of the head of John the Baptist, tradition has it that in 1016, the monks of Saint-Jean-d'Angély in the Aquitaine discovered the head of John. When the head was exhibited, many thousands of people, from Italy to Spain, hurried to the place. Nobility gathered there, offering precious gifts of varied sorts. For example, the king of the Franks gave a bowl of pure gold weighing thirty pounds and precious draperies made of silk and gold for the decoration of the church.

THE ATTRACTION OF THE CROSS

There's a far more biblical way to attract people to church. Jesus said, "And I, if I am lifted up from the earth, will draw all men to Myself" (John 12:32). Here Jesus is speaking of the worldwide appeal His victory will have over the forces of evil and especially of the appeal that His death will have in drawing people of every nation, tongue, and tribe to Himself. *Jesus doesn't call us to attract people to our churches. He calls us to minister the gospel through which He attracts people to Himself.* This is what men have forgotten today: the inherent power of the cross to draw people to Jesus!

These days, men think long and hard about how to attract people to their churches while failing to understand how it is that Christ attracts people to Himself. The manmade decoys of modern marketing, and its sideshows, pale before the power of the cross of Christ to appeal to the sinner's heart. Many years ago, a young Seminarian asked me, "How do I preach the cross?" I replied, "The Cross preaches itself. God has put *power* in the message of the Cross. Lift up Jesus with unction from on high, and the rest will take care of itself."

The developing tendency among the churches is not to lift up Christ crucified so that His stripes, wounds, and bloodied brow can be clearly seen. It's to diminish the cross for fear that our churches might not appear attractive. But that's the Church. We're a bloody mess. We're washed in blood. Jesus said to Thomas, "Reach here with your finger, and see My hands; and reach here your hand and put it into My side; and do not be unbelieving, but believing" (John 20:27). This is the answer for the doubting Thomases of the world: the biblical exposition of the passion and death of Christ.

There's Power in the Blood

The attractiveness of the cross is especially manifest in its convicting power. Did you know that the cross is God's opinion of you in your sinfulness? You can't reflect on the cross of Jesus without also bearing in mind God's immense anger over every sin you've ever committed. The level of God's rage is immeasurable. The flood of Noah's day, the destruction of Sodom, all the plagues of Egypt, can't begin to match the level of Divine fury Jesus endured the day He hung on Calvary's cross for our sins. The very thought ought to convict you of your sins and attract you to it where there is forgiveness, full and free. The apostle Paul declares, "For the word of the cross is foolishness to those who are perishing, but to us who are being saved, it is the power of God" (1 Corinthians 1:18).

Christ's Sufferings, More Than the Law Demanded

There's a related truth to be gleaned from the passion of our Lord which brings out its attractiveness all the more. While it's common to say that Jesus died for our sins—and indeed He did—consider this: when the police find a dead body they call it "murder." But should they discover a brutal slaying, someone who died as a result of either being beaten over and over again, or stabbed repeatedly, or perhaps shot multiple times, investigators call it "a crime of passion." When a crime of passion occurs, law enforcement can safely assume that the assailant was likely someone very close to the deceased.

Now let's apply these facts to the death of Christ. The Law only required the death of an innocent animal for the expiation of sins. But reflect on the passion of Christ, and instantly you will see that His was not a mere death, as is commonly thought. What he suffered was more akin to a crime of passion. Over the course of hours, Jesus' body was brutalized, ripped, shredded, nailed to a cross, and left to die in agonizing pain.

Now there's one thing we know about this grizzly death: the assailant was someone very close to the deceased. For the One who poured out all of heavens' fury that dreadful day at Golgatha was Jesus' own Father. And yet there is a further point to contemplate. The Father's inestimable rage, though endured by the Son, was meant for you and me. We were the ones to whom not only the stroke was due, but also the torrents of unmitigated brutality. Our sins angered God to such an extent that He desired to brutalize us over the course of many hours before allowing us to die in anguish. But instead we have received grace and mercy. Were it not for the grace of God, we most assuredly would have undergone the same fateful end Jesus bore.

To think that the Son endured not only our death penalty for breaking God's laws, but also the violence of the Father's wrath, causes the grace and mercy of God toward us to shine forth brighter than the noonday sun. Are you now beginning to see the attraction of the cross? Can you think of an innovation in ministry that is more compelling than this?

THE ELEPHANT IN THE ROOM

Why have many evangelical pastors abandoned the message of the cross in favor of innovation in ministry? *They no longer believe in the power of the Gospel!* If asked, virtually every minister would affirm the power of the gospel. But then weigh his answer against what you actually see and hear coming from the pulpit. Do you see an impassioned preacher declaring the Scriptures in all their purity and power? Do you sense that he stands in the gap between a holy God and lost sinners as he calls a fallen world to repentance and faith? Do you hear in his voice the urgency to come to Christ in order to escape the judgment of God? Does he plead the blood of Christ, the cross of Christ, or the grace of Christ for sinners? If not, then what do you think he believes in his heart about sin, redemption, and belief?

The fabric of gospel preaching and teaching is moth-eaten because we have hidden it deep in our church closets and left it there too long. We've done so because we are ashamed to be seen in such old clothes. We're embarrassed by the gospel. In its place we wear the fashionable messages of the world, hoping that their newness will appeal to modern sensitivities. But it's all a lie of the devil. Not until we are *un*ashamed of the gospel will God be pleased.

Talk Is Not Enough

I once discussed the lack of gospel-centeredness in our churches with another pastor. He remarked, "John, I don't know what you mean. In each and every worship service we talk about Jesus." But dear reader, I say to you, as I pointed out to my friend, there's a world of difference between talking about Jesus and preaching Christ. To *preach* Christ is not to talk about how Jesus is the answer for your mid-life crisis. To preach Christ is to preach the realities of sin, salvation, heaven, hell, His passion, the glorious grace of God to sinners as repentance from sin, trust alone on Christ for the forgiveness of sins, and holiness of living.

THE IMPOSING SHADOW OF NEO-LIBERALISM

The apprehensiveness in both the pulpit and the pew toward the clear and radical meaning of the gospel has provided for the rise of a *new secularism* within Protestant evangelical Christianity. In effect, we have become *ad hoc* liberals. During the early-nineteenth century, the tenets of liberalism that eventually destroyed many mainline denominations first emerged in Old Testament studies. They quickly spread to New Testament studies and were strengthened in the early-twentieth century through the influence of Darwinism. During the mid-twentieth century, liberalism expanded yet again in the area of the philosophy of religion with the likes of Paul Tillich and the influence of existentialism.

Now in the twenty-first century, the threat to orthodox Christian belief is coming from a different location on the theological spectrum—practical theology. This includes the areas of church growth, church development, and missions. But in distinction from the older form of liberalism, this new influence isn't coming from the old denominational seminaries. It's emerging from within our very own so-called "conservative" evangelical churches and schools of learning. What is motivating the secularization of evangelicalism? The root cause of our departing the faith once delivered to the saints is the avarice to be big.

The outcome of *ad hoc* liberalism has given us scores of churches full of *unregenerate believers*. These are people who believe everything but experience nothing. The presence and power of the Holy Spirit is missing from their lives. They're not true Christians. Paul warned that the last days will be marked by men "holding to a form of godliness, although they have denied its power" (2 Timothy 3:5). Inspect the more popular approaches to church planting, church growth, evangelism, and missions, and you'll notice they are full of demographics, 5-year plans, and guaranteed percentages—everything but power. The Church can get along without charts and graphs, but it can't exist without power. Without the power of the cross and the power of the Holy Spirit in ministry, what else do we expect to produce but a bumper crop of unregenerate believers?

The subject of this chapter provides a natural link to the next—the unpardonable state of preaching in so many of our churches.

4

What to Feed Your Living Bible

"Let us rejoice with one another that in a world where there are a great many good and happy things for men to do, God has given us the best and happiest, and made us preachers of His Truth."

—PHILLIPS BROOKS

THE EARLY '70S MARKED the beginning of my earnest investigation into the claims of Christ. Since the teachings of Jesus are in the Bible, one of the first things I did was pick up a copy of the *Living Bible*. It read pretty well, so I kept reading. Then one day I found a copy of the *King James Version* of the Bible and began to read it. As I did, I couldn't help but notice great differences between what it recorded and what I had read in the pages of *The Living Bible*.

Now my purpose here is not to debunk *The Living Bible*. The book has served its intended goal for many years and will no doubt continue to be a source of comfort and encouragement to people for years to come. Notwithstanding this fact, there is little question that *The Living Bible* doesn't say what the original text says. It's a paraphrase of the Bible in the contemporary jargon of modern man. But because it doesn't say what God said to holy men of old, the real meaning of the original text is unclear.

With the birth and spread of the market-driven church, preaching and teaching have also taken on the characteristic of not saying what the Bible says. As a consequence, spiritual matters aren't clarified, they are muddied.

The reader may not be engaged in preaching or teaching on a regular basis; nonetheless, let me encourage you to keep reading. I believe you'll find in these pages some shocking details which require your full attention.

The Easy Pulpit

The problem of preachers not preaching what the Bible says crystallized in my mind when I attended a special seminar conducted by the senior pastor of a mega-church. At some point, after already making a number of shocking comments regarding ministry, he turned to the students in the room, and referring to his own preaching, proudly declared, "We never say anything about sin!" Once I got my jaw up off the floor, my unspoken thought was, "Well I guess that's how you build a mega-church. Don't say anything about sin." What may have been even more shocking was that no one in attendance questioned his remark.

This is the new trend. Don't say anything about sin, the blood, the cross, the dangers of hell, or the crucified life. Just keep it light. Why? It's all part of a larger strategy. The modernized church feeds off the sinner's innate desire for a *gentler, kinder image of God*. It meets this desire by tickling people's ears.

Is Your Doctor Killing You?

The minister who says, "We never say anything about sin" is the same minister who never says anything about the gospel. How can people know the extent of the answer, which is the grace of God in salvation, unless they are told the extent of the problem, which is sin? The new sensibility is to skirt the hard truths revolving around sin for fear of ruffling feathers and offending secular pluralists. But a competent physician wouldn't say, "I don't want to offend my patient so I'm not going to tell him he has cancer." If a doctor wants to save his patient's life, he'll tell him the truth regarding his condition and then hold out the remedy. Similarly, people everywhere are dying from a disease far worse than cancer. It's sin. Cancer can only kill the body. But sin kills the soul. How much more is the preacher of God's Word under obligation to warn his patient of the peril posed by sin and point him to the Savior's healing balm!

To Whom Are You Indebted?

Paul was a man who described himself as being under a certain obligation to preach the gospel. In Romans 1:14, he records, "I am under obligation both to Greeks and to barbarians." Now the Greeks and barbarians have not loaned Paul anything which they expect him to pay back. So what does he owe them? The following verse provides the answer. "So, for my part, I am eager to preach the gospel." Paul's obligation, or his debt, is to preach the gospel. God's grace to Paul has made him a debtor to others— to tell them of the consequences of their sin and the grace of God in salvation. That is what Paul focuses on in verse 15, where he states, "We have received grace and apostleship." So Paul is under obligation to the world of sinners, and what he owes them is the full gospel. Grace doesn't make you a debtor to God, but it does make you a debtor to others who also are in need of grace.

The preacher is most certainly under obligation to tell people about their true spiritual condition—that apart from Christ they are dead in their trespasses and sins and that salvation is found in no other place than in the grace of God. He must declare with great passion and compelling love, "Look, you've broken God's laws and right now you're a criminal in God's sight. And He's out to bring you to justice." But then he will hold out the answer: the cure for sin, which is found in Christ Jesus alone.

I'm not saying that the new craze is to avoid mention of sin altogether. However, even where sin is talked about, its typically the *general concept* of sin, not specific sins, that are discussed, for fear that someone in the congregation might be practicing them and may be offended at their mention. Dare we keep people from the grace of God because we were too timid to tell them of their sin? Perish the thought!

I once heard a popular preacher claim he doesn't expound on the subject of sin because he doesn't want to "dwell on the negative." Mothers, please remember the words of this preacher. The next time your child is sick with a high fever be sure not to give him or her bitter-tasting medicine that will facilitate healing. After all, you don't want to dwell on the negative.

Truths to Evade

As well as being disturbingly silent on the significant issues of man's sinfulness before a holy God, and God's gracious salvation in Christ, there are many other subjects the modish pulpit seeks to avoid. While these topics are too numerous to name, they share a common denominator. They have the potential to generate controversy. In the evangelical church of today, controversial statements are to be avoided like the plague. They are potentially dangerous, in as much as they can divide people, the very thing to steer clear of when trying to build a larger church. *The #1 enemy of the stylish pulpit is controversial statements.*

Controversial statements come in various shapes and sizes, but typically they appear in two forms: biblical and cultural. To avoid controversial, biblical statements, sermons are to be kept awash in the naiveté of warm sentiment so as not to infer incrimination, or worse, to sound judgmental. Things especially to be avoided would be statements that might sound dogmatic. This includes the clear exposition of Bible texts, references to God's Law, and the word "ought." And never, ever, point fingers. Challenging Bible stories are to be softened with anecdotes from pop culture, producing messages that are broadly ingratiating and that encourage people to "look up." Bible studies and Sunday school lessons, so as not to appear doctrinaire, are to de-emphasize the meaning of Scripture passages in favor of giving equal validity to everyone's opinion.

Then there are those hot-button cultural issues. Abortion, homosexuality, illegal immigration, and the war against terror should all be sidestepped in order to appear "above it all"—a phrase which, in evangelical parlance, is tantamount to being godly. Sadly, the result of this twaddle is that people in the pews are being fed little more than an insipid set of moralisms about faith, family, and extended relationships. *The evangelical pulpit is quickly becoming synonymous with virtuous mediocrity.*

When former President Ronald Reagan stood before the Brandenburg Gate of the Berlin Wall and said, "Mr. Gorbachev, tear down this wall!" his remarks were greeted by the liberal U. S. media with rolled eyes and smirks. "There he goes again!" they decried. Yet Reagan's strong stand proved to be a key turning point in the Cold War. Unfortunately, firmness to stand on principle and not to allow oneself to get swept up in the tide of public sentiment seems to be the very thing missing from the popular pulpit. It's become so hung up on not offending that it fails to say what God has commanded. This erosion is not merely one of gospel values, but also strikes at the very vitality of the life of the Church.

NEED FOR GREATER REFORMATION

The chic pulpit of today doubles as the psychiatrist's couch. Disorders, diseases, and addictions replace sin, while recovery takes the place of confession, repentance, and daily obedience. This is not to say that all evangelical pulpits have abandoned the power of the gospel as THE means to help people conquer their problems. A good many pastors, in fact, are clear on the role of daily repentance and faith in overcoming daily tribulations. While I certainly applaud this fact, permit me to suggest that such preachers still may not have gone far enough to reform the pulpit.

The real difference between the message of Christianity and the message of the self-help gurus isn't the difference between using secular therapeutic methods to overcome your problems verses using biblical confession and repentance to overcome your problems. *The difference is seen in the fact that Jesus came to overcome us!*

According to the Bible, we don't have a problem. We *are* the problem. Jesus doesn't offer Himself as the answer to life's problems. He calls us to Himself, *in whom* is life itself. He bids, "Come to Me, all who are weary and heavy-laden, and I will give you rest. Take My yoke upon you and learn from Me, for I am gentle and humble in heart, and you will find rest for your souls. For My yoke is easy and My burden is light" (Matthew 11:28–30). To the extent that we abide in Him, and He in us, the remaining stain of sin is removed, and life's pressures fade from sight.

A Case from History

There is historical precedent for the present unhealthy tendency in the evangelical pulpit. During the seventeenth century, a great deal of debate surfaced among Dutch pastors over the dual issue of the total depravity of man and God's electing purposes in Christ. This debate resulted from the fear that taking too hard a stand on these, and related, doctrinal positions could create division within the Protestant movement and ultimately chase people away from the churches.

In a sincere effort to bring all men of good will together in Christ, Moses Amyraut produced the doctrine of "hypothetical universalism."

This is the dual idea that God decreed to save every man in Christ on condition of faith, but in the light of His particular decree, wills to save only some. In other words, this is the odd teaching that Jesus Christ died for all men, but only the elect in Christ receive the benefits of His work through faith. Amyraut's effort produced a humanized account of God and kicked off a long series of efforts by both theologians and philosophers of doctrinal minimalism.

A similar move swept the Church of post-restoration England (after 1660). Largely under the influence of the Cambridge Platonists, broadmindedness in doctrinal issues literally snowballed and spread far beyond the particular issues of man's sinfulness and God's saving grace.

Reacting mainly against the Puritans, and theologically broad in outlook, John Tillotson, Archbishop of Canterbury, led a group of Anglican clergy who, aligning themselves with the stylish and liberal movements in the enlightened intellectual world, pleaded for a degree of "latitude" in matters of interpreting and preaching the Scriptures. They thus took as their proud title, "latitudinarians." Their goal was to resist the High Church insistence on conformity in nonessentials, choosing instead to take great liberty in the order of congregational worship and to harmonize Scripture with the "light of reason." These practices normally meant that congregational worship in general, and sermons and writings in particular, were strongly moralistic in tone, yet theologically vague and spiritually insubstantial enough so that just about everyone could feel at ease.

Strongly moralistic in tone? Theologically vague and spiritually insubstantial enough so that just about everyone could feel at ease? Overall, this is the shape of evangelical preaching and teaching today.

THE BIBLICAL MANDATE FOR BOLD PROCLAMATION

Conversely, Elijah was a man of God who never backed down from preaching what God said. In 2 Kings 6, we find the king of Aram, likely Ben-Hadad II, about to come up against Jehoram, the king of Israel. This is not a full-scale war, but one of many border skirmishes that were common during this period. When the king of Aram planned to camp against the king of Israel, the man of God sent word to Jehoram more than once of impending disaster should he go by the place where the enemy was camped. Elijah said to the King, "Beware that you do not pass this place, for the Arameans are coming down there" (v. 9). The king of

Israel listened to Elijah and was protected from disaster on more than one occasion (v. 10). Elisha did not present the King a rhetorical homily or a feel-good sermon, nor did he water-down the eminent danger facing him to make him feel at ease. He told it like it was.

Likewise, the man of God who fills the pulpit must tell it like it is. He must proclaim, "Sir, beware that if you keep hanging near that married women, if you go by this place, the devil is waiting." Young person, "Beware, if you get caught up in this material culture, if you pass by this place, the devil is lurking." In all cases, he must point people to the safety of the cross.

There was a day in America when pulpits thundered with warnings that should you pass by this place, a trap is waiting. You heard of sin, redemption, heaven, hell, holiness, and much more. And we weren't afraid to apply the Bible to touchy social subjects like politics, the evils of homosexuality and abortion, and to call people to living radical lives for Jesus in the public square. But this time of revival fire is quickly dimming. It's a failure of nerve. Truth be told, *we have already arrived at a time when those that still wish to live radical lives for Jesus are perceived as a greater threat to the life of the Church than those who live in open sin.*

So what ought to be the preacher's true objectives? I'll cover several rather briefly.

SOME THOUGHTS ON PREACHING

The most important goal of preaching is first and always the person and work of Jesus Christ. God doesn't expect His servants to proclaim temporal happiness, how Jesus wants them to be all that God intended them to be, or principles of earthly success. He expects them to preach precisely what the Bible states: no more, no less. From the Bible, though numerous truths will arise depending on the exact text in view, ultimately the preacher must declare Christ. Paul said of his public ministry, "For I determined to know nothing among you except Jesus Christ, and Him crucified" (1 Corinthians 2:2).

The person and work of Christ is the central message of every passage of Scripture. Christ is the Bible's subject and object. It's been said, "Touch the Bible anywhere and you touch Christ somewhere." From Genesis to Revelation, the person and work of Christ is the main thread running through the Bible's entire system of theology. Jesus said, "For if you believed Moses, you would believe Me, for he wrote about Me"

(John 5:46). Whether the text is from 1 Corinthians, or 1 Chronicles, chapter 1, Christ is to be preached and exalted. Regardless of the cultural pressures to perform otherwise, let the preacher announce Christ's perfect life for sinners, His death for sinners, His resurrection for sinners, and His sovereign power to build His Church, and His coming again for His Church.

We may preach the significance and attractiveness of brotherly relationships, the temporal benefits of salvation, the all-importance of faith, and even the promise of new spiritual bodies without pain or defect. Yet, in the final analysis these biblical themes and directives always bring us back to the core message of the Bible, who is Christ—His glorious person and finished work. Whether we preach a Bible story, psalm, proverb, or biblical narrative, the call of the preacher is to divide the Word and bring out, as from behind a veil, the Christ of Scripture.

We must preach Christ, declare Christ, magnify Christ, and glorify Christ. He is the "treasure hidden in the field," and the "pearl of great price," for which a man sold all that he had in order to purchase for his own. To preach Christ is the surest way to say what the Bible says.

When I think of how much evangelical preaching and teaching should honor and exalt Christ, I am reminded of the poignant words of St. Patrick, who said,

> Christ be with me, Christ within me, Christ behind me, Christ before me, Christ beside me, Christ to win me, Christ to comfort and restore me, Christ beneath me, Christ above me, Christ in quiet, Christ in danger, Christ in hearts of all that love me, Christ in mind of friend and stranger.

And by all means, dear preacher, do not preach as though there's not enough wind of the Spirit to fill your lungs so as to make you appear as a listless mannequin before your listeners. Not all men preach with the fiery and golden oratory of a John Chrysostom, George Whitefield, Billy Graham, D. James Kennedy, or John Hagee. However, the answer to the pretentious, hyped-up, theatrical presentations called Christian worship services isn't preaching so dry that congregants feel as though they need No-Doze to stay awake during the sermon. Preach filled with Holy Spirit unction, with heart-felt understanding of your text, and you'll preach with such a holy boldness that the sheer manifestation of the presence and power of the Spirit coming from the pulpit will encourage among your listeners more zeal for Christ than all the moralistic, self-help messages together could ever hope to achieve.

Second, always preach evangelistically with Holy Spirit passion for the lost. Do you automatically assume that all who hear your sermons are born-again Christians? Or do you prepare your sermons with the lost in mind? It's a stunning fact that within two generations after the Puritans and Separatists settled New England, the land in which they had hoped to create a visible expression of the Kingdom of God on earth was already in need of revival. Spiritual conditions were so poor that even many pastors held to nominal belief. Jonathan Edwards (1703–1758), George Whitefield (1714–1770), and Gilbert Tennent (1703–1764)—all major figures in America's First Great Awakening—addressed the dangers of unconverted clergymen.

During this period it was common to find many pastors preaching moralistically, associating the Christian life with little more than outward conformity to the Sermon on the Mount or loving one's neighbor as themselves. Absent was clear teaching on the depravity of man, the reality of hell, and the necessity of faith and repentance. The accumulation of unconverted pastors was an institutional problem in eighteenth-century New England.

As preachers, we assume that most, if not all, who hear us on a Sunday morning are Christians in need of further training and assurance. I recall a conversation I had with the late Dr. Bill Bright regarding what he termed the problem of a "lack of assurance of salvation" among many congregants in the established churches of California after World War II. This is one reason Bright spent the time he did crafting materials aimed at providing Christians assurance of their salvation. But I have often wondered, "Did these church members lack assurance of their salvation because they were never really saved?"

Surely the plethora of people within our churches guilty of fornication, adultery, internet pornography—much of which has lead to struggling or failed marriages—the great reluctance of people to serve diligently on church boards, and the near dearth of people willing to engage in personal evangelism ought to point to an underlying cause we haven't taken the time to consider seriously. Perhaps many of these people simply aren't believers. This is why every sermon must herald the salvation of Christ, boldly and without compromise. No shallow moralisms that make people feel good, but which fail to strike at the conscience and the heart.

Each sermon must reveal the terror of God's condemnation on all those who've fallen short of His Law, followed by the grace of God in Christ. Appeal to the conscience, painting vivid pictures from Scripture of your hearers' lost condition. Depend on the power of God's Word to cause sincere anxiety in your listeners over the condition of their souls before the Holy God of heaven and earth, urging them to put away their sin and come to Christ for sanctuary. Visit Mt. Sinai first. Then take your hearers to Mt. Calvary where there's everlasting relief and joy. And always preach for a verdict! If you're not a preacher, and your preacher isn't preaching evangelistically, get yourself another preacher!

Third, always make your preaching depend solely on the sovereignty of God. Jesus said, "You did not choose Me but I chose you" (John 15:16). God's sovereignty in redemption procures for the preacher unquenchable confidence that whether he preaches from the pulpit or shares the love of Christ with people he meets throughout the week, God's people are out there, and when they hear the Word of the Lord, they will respond in kind (Isaiah 55:11).

But rather than rely on God's sovereign grace in the heralding of the Good News, far too many of us have come to depend on the force of our personalities in the pulpit to sway people's hearts and minds God-ward. Preachers act this way out of their belief that unless non-Christians cast their vote for God, God remains in heaven with His hands tied. It thus falls to the preacher to be the salesman, to use whatever devices are at his disposal to prod, coax, and convince people to accept Jesus. But the gospel is powerful, not on the basis of the wit, charm, and conventions of the preacher, but because God causes it to be so.

Men lack boldness in their preaching because they have no real confidence in God's sovereign power to save the lost. Feeling uncertain, even fearful, of what people will think of the message, they hold back from declaring heaven's ultimatum. Unless we preachers regain a biblical embrace of the fact that it's God who calls people to Himself, preaching will remain humanistic in nature and generally powerless to lead people to conviction of sin, repentance, and faith.

Third, never allow yourself to feel puffed-up by your ability to preach. I recall as a young preacher being rather enthralled with my ability to keep the attention of a crowded room. You'll know you're full of yourself before, and during, the sermon when after the sermon you're not concerned to hear how your message prompted a need for righteous living among your listeners, but instead your only joy is to hear what a great job you did. Having learned of the treachery of my own deceitful heart, I now say two things to myself just before entering the pulpit by way of preparation.

First, I say, "God, I can't do it without you." There's just something about this little phrase which reminds me not to rely on anything in myself for the delivery of the message, but to lean solely on God.

The second thing I say to myself is, "John, minister." This phrase helps me shift my focus from the technical aspects of preaching to being a vessel through whom God can minister His Word. It really helps.

Finally, be a man of prayer. One of the greatest preachers of the nineteenth century was Robert Murray McCheyne (1813–1843). In 1840, three years before his death, he wrote to a seminary student to give this bit of advice, "Above all, keep much in the presence of God. Never see the face of man till you have seen His face who is our life, our all. Pray for others, pray for your teachers, fellow students." [1]

In his book, *Joy Unspeakable*, Dr. Martyn Lloyd-Jones recounts the powerful effect prayer had in the ministry of McCheyne, who after spending much time with God in prayer, merely had to walk out and face his congregation and a spirit of repentance would sweep the room. "It has been authenticated so many, many times, that Robert Murray McCheyne had simply to enter the pulpit and before he had opened his mouth people used to begin to weep and were convicted of sin. He had not uttered a word. Why? Well, the explanation was that this man had come from the presence of God and the Spirit was poured forth."[2] Are you an empty vessel? Do you spend time each day in prayer, seeking the anointing of the Holy Spirit on your preaching?

Building up the Body of Christ entails more than the preaching and teaching of the Word of God. It also includes the terribly overlooked area of church discipline.

---

1. Andrew A. Bonar, *The Biography of Robert Murray McCheyne* (Edinburgh: Banner of Truth, 1960), 46.

2. Martyn Lloyd-Jones, *Joy Unspeakable*, 4th ed. (Wheaton: Harold Shaw Publishers, 1988) 119.

5

The Evangelical Resolution Against Church Discipline and Other Cruel, Inhumane, and Degrading Treatment

"Discipline is the soul of an army. It makes small numbers formidable, procures success to the weak, and esteem to all.

—George Washington

WOULD YOU SUPPORT THE waterboarding of a terrorist if you thought you could elicit crucial information that could save thousands of lives? This question, which is the child of 9/11 and the subsequent war against terror, causes us to reflect on how far we're willing to go in order to spare the lives of innocent people.

How far we're willing to go to save people's lives is also a pertinent question for church life. So let's reframe our previous question this way. Would you support the banning of a Christian brother from the Lord's Table if you thought you could get him to stop committing adultery? Would you even go as far as to support his excommunication from the church if it meant turning his life around?

Now remember, a life hangs in the balance. The Bible is quite clear that those who practice adultery will have no place in God's kingdom (1 Corinthians 6:9). And even though your friend may have made a public profession of faith, and even though he may be a member of the church, the direction of his life now says otherwise. How far are you willing to go to save the life of your friend?

Unfortunately, the new fad within evangelicalism is to downplay the important role of church discipline in the serious matters of the heart. The very thought of providing stern correction to a wayward congregant, even if it be for the purpose of bringing him to repentance, is increasingly viewed as "way harsh." The alternative, we are told, is to show love not judgment. In time, the offender will come around.

WHY CHURCH DISCIPLINE IS DECLINING

There is evidence that the proper exercise of church discipline has been falling off in many churches and denominations for years. At a time when the number of divorces is escalating within the community of believers, when people are permitted to just "walk away" from their church membership vows and are dropped from the rolls, when known unbelievers are openly permitted to partake in the Lord's Supper, and when many reject any objective moral code, little, if anything, is being done to provide responsible Christian nurture and counsel. Accordingly, our churches are more and more being compromised by various forms of sin. As the late Dr. D. James Kennedy once remarked, "Church discipline is dead as the Dodo bird."

It's true that many pressures claim the time of church staff, making it difficult for them to be aware of every issue within the congregation. As a result, many are simply unaware of problems. Could this really be the only thing keeping us from our biblical duty to insist on church discipline procedures? The sad reality is that an unspiritual tendency has emerged within the churches, one in which leaders and laymen alike are showing resistance to the very idea of church discipline. Why is this unfortunate pattern emerging?

The problem people have with biblically prescribed church discipline flows from their deeper problem with God's justice. Since the Garden of Eden, all people are born with an inbred, spiritual tendency to "buck authority." Our natural and sinful urge is toward rugged individualism, to be the master of our own destiny.

We see this ungodly pattern in the human heart as early as the creation account. In Genesis 3 we find two trees: the tree of life and the tree of the knowledge of good and evil. The tree of life stands for eternal life. To eat of its fruit gives one the gift of everlasting years. It points to the cross. Jesus hung upon a tree. Look to the cross, eat of its fruit, and you will receive eternal life. The tree of the knowledge of good and evil however, doesn't mean that before the Fall Adam knew only good, so when he ate of the fruit, his eyes were opened to know the difference between good and evil. This tree stands for determining what is good or bad for one's self, apart from God's Word. It signifies seeking knowledge in human independence from God.

The Manipulation Game

Rugged individualism is now manifestly present in many churches and is spreading to others. To a greater extent, congregants desire forgiveness without standards, compassion without correction, and blessing without responsibility. Unfortunately, plenty of church leaders, rather than teach the constructive aspects of church discipline, are now trying to flatter this tendency, believing that properly manipulated, it can provide needed energy for building big numbers. They operate on the wrongheaded assumption that people can be enticed to remain in a church by simply exploiting their individualistic desire not to be judged.

Some pastors instinctively know that people will automatically have a visceral reaction if even a brief air of authority should permeate the church, so they purposely downplay the need for formal discipline and the ecclesiastical authority by which discipline functions. To quote the prophet, they have purposely made themselves like "mute dogs unable to bark, dreamers lying down, who love to slumber" (Isa. 56:10). In the restructured church-of-today, the term "submission" is a 4-letter word. Of course no one will admit this. No, the propaganda is to say that we are a church that seeks to "do church differently."

Justice and Mercy Together

People who are at issue with God's justice need to understand that without justice at work in the Church, there's no possibility for God's mercy. Here's a simple analogy. In the sphere of education, a teacher would be foolish to reward lack of learning and bad test scores with good grades. Assessment of students should proceed along the lines of justice: good performance in learning ought to be rewarded with a good assessment. This is simply another way of saying that the foundation in education is justice. Another name for it may be truth. To credit excellent class work with an excellent grade is to proceed along the lines of truth. You're calling it what it is. Likewise, to evaluate poor work with a poor grade is to follow truth: you're calling class work what it is.

When the foundation of justice and truth is established in education, the prospect of mercy is created. For example, if a teacher calls poor class work, poor, that teacher can respond in mercy and go beyond the demands of justice by staying after school to help the struggling student. But if the foundation of truth and justice are abandoned, then mercy has no meaning, because mercy means going beyond what justice requires.

The same ideas apply within the Body of Christ. If we as church leaders aren't willing to call bad behavior, bad behavior, and hold people's feet to the fire, then we will not be motivated to go beyond the demands of God's just standards and apply mercy, which is embodied in the process of church discipline. And unless church members are willing to submit to the discipline of the Church, then they have effectively removed themselves from under the redemptive cover of God's mercy.

God's mercy in the lives of God's people is never more clearly evident than when the Church seeks to win back the wayward soul through the appropriate channels of church discipline. It's a quirk of irony that the Christian who seeks after a church that only speaks of love and not the chastising hand of God is really seeking after a mirror that reflects a god of his own making, one in whom there is no real love or mercy.

Manic Individualism

The issue people have with God's justice is manifestly evident in the extreme subjectivism of the age. One example of such extreme subjectivism is the neo-anarchist movement. Modern anarchism takes its cue from a philosophical movement which, despite representatives who don't share a completely unified approach, generally advocates replacing the authority of the state with participants freely developing their own sense of morality, ethics, and behavior.

Perhaps the reader has noticed a capital A with a circle around it somewhere on his or her child's arm or leg? The circled A is the sign of the anarchist movement. The advance of anarchism is gaining momentum in schools with kids as young as elementary school level. It's not uncommon to see very young students embrace images and priorities that celebrate death, the macabre, extreme introspection, and the outright rejection of social norms.

Judge Not?

Associated with society's message of extreme subjectivism is the philosophy of non-judgmentalism. Politically-correct, liberal humanism, says, "Don't judge anyone!" Instead, we are to live in a "judgment-free zone." Humanism tries to beat it into our heads. Tolerance of people's choices, not discernment, is what matters. Freethinking, not stereotypes. What is right for one person may not be right for another. There are no absolute standards, just whatever turns your crank. The very atmosphere that elitist, sophisticated, liberal secularism seeks to create opposes the very notion of critical judgment.

THE NEW IDEAL

In recent years, the move toward both secularism and subjectivism in the Western world has intensified the challenge to the churches to reformulate their view of government and the oversight of their ministries from the juridical approach, concentrated on authority, to the *therapeutic managerial church model.* According to this model, church discipline officiated by the ministers of a church is replaced with amiable relationships among the people as the key means to keep folks in check and to safeguard the purity of the congregations. This approach, alluded to at the top of the chapter, sees censure and love as mutually exclusive. Anything more than praying for, and loving the sinner back to spiritual health, is interpreted as draconian.

An Easy Excuse

The ease with which secularization and subjectivism breached the walls of our churches and supplanted official discipline with the therapeutic managerial church model was also made possible by a growing suspicion of formal *church government* within these same churches. Church discipline and church government are inseparably linked insofar as church government provides the formal context for the discipline of church members.

Rather than embrace the offices of the church as Christ-ordained, at some point, the new trend became to mentally identify ecclesiastical government as a relic from the medieval past and to brand any attempt to retain it as synonymous with a Fortune-500 company's intoxication with corporate administration. Once church government came under increased scrutiny, its little cousin—church discipline—was not far behind.

No Need to Polarize

I would be foolish to suggest that church discipline can function apart from filial associations. In fact, the practice of reconciling people, as outlined in Matthew 18:15–17 begins with self-regulating relationships. The initial phases of the steps to peace-making require the offended person to go to the offender and attempt to reconcile at that level. If he or she is unwilling to listen, two or three concerned Christians (those with first-hand knowledge of the offense) are to become involved in confronting the offender. These steps assume the significant contribution personal relationships can, and should, play in reconciliation and in protecting the peace of a local church. Also, they seek to avoid the formal church disciplinary process. But convivial associations aren't meant as a substitute for the involvement of the role of sanctioned church courts and the potential inclusion of the whole congregation in resolving disputes. *Christian love is not the reverse of official discipline. A church can have both.*

Clearly, our corporate bodily life together suffers from a concrete lack of understanding of what the Bible says about church discipline, especially its *positive* intent. Let's look into it.

THE PURPOSE OF CHURCH DISCIPLINE

Church discipline embraces two aspects of church life: *formative discipline* and *corrective discipline*. Formative discipline seeks to grow people in the image of Christ, bringing them to maturity, the way a football coach might discipline his team through daily practices and workouts. To be a "disciple" of Jesus Christ means having a commitment to Bible study, prayer, church attendance, learning what is right and wrong, and receiving the Word through preaching, the sacraments, Sunday school classes, private study, formal training, and more. A local church carries out formative discipline through its ministries.

Corrective discipline—which is the main focus of this chapter, and which I shall refer to from this point on as "church discipline"—is also a practice that rests upon the divine authority of the Bible and is vital to the purity, power, peace, and progress of the Church. In fact, without the presence of church discipline, and the required church courts to carry out this vital function, a church simply doesn't exist. While it's become popular to suggest that all people have to do is meet together under the banner of Christ's name in order to establish a new church, a church doesn't exist unless what exists bears the signs of the Church, not least of which is the necessary arrangement by which, and through which, the exercise of discipline may be achieved.

Certainly, the Scriptures record, "For where two or three have gathered together in My name, I am there in their midst" (Matthew 18:20). However, that Christ is in our midst doesn't mean a church is in our midst. While a church can't exist unless Christ is present to fill it, the presence of Christ in the midst of two to three people isn't enough to create a church. For a true church to be existent, the "signs" of a church must be present. The responsibility and necessity for the sign of church discipline isn't an option for those who claim to regularly associate as a church. Christians who obey the Word of God must be equally committed to carefully following this practice.

In brief, church discipline has three purposes in view.

First, church discipline aims to honor Christ. The Bible is clear that Jesus Christ is the Head of the Church (Colossians 1:24 and Ephesians 5:25–27). Because Jesus is the Head of the Church, everything done within each church must seek to honor Him. First and foremost, the goal of spiritual correction isn't the welfare of people, but the interests of the Lord's reputation. Though no one's walk with the Lord is without sin, the Church is not to sanction sin. This means that those that embrace sin as a practice are *not* to be treated as Christians, for to do so is to dishonor Christ.

The Church mustn't coddle profane and incorrigible members without some shame falling upon its Head. The world waits to denounce the truth of Christ like a wolf waits in ready to pounce upon its prey. The sight of habitual offenders and outright scandal within the Christian church are to the world what the slightest smell of a weak and helpless animal is to the hungry wolf. He will rip its carcass thinking he's getting to Christ. In recent years, key evangelical leaders, whose notorious behavior has shocked the world, have provided the worldly wolf numerous opportunities to attack and lacerate the body of Christ in the hopes of inflicting greater damage upon Christ Himself. Carefully and prayerfully administered discipline serves to frustrate this evil scheme.

Second, church discipline seeks to protect the peace and purity of the Church.

As the Bible so wisely records, "Do not be deceived: 'Bad company corrupts good morals'" (1 Corinthians 15:33). Good Christians are kept safe from the contamination of immoral men when the corrupt are corrected or even removed from fellowship by discipline. For this reason it's also imperative that the upright in heart do their best to avoid close associations with an unrepentant offender who's been removed from a congregation. It's with foresight of danger to the godly that Paul writes with a heavy hand to the Church at Corinth to expel an incestuous man from their company (1 Corinthians 5:11).

The exercise of church discipline also serves to send a clear signal throughout the whole congregation that anyone even thinking of spreading false teaching should think twice (Titus 1:10–11). From the example God made of those caught up in Korah's rebellion (Numbers 16) to the swift and sure judgment of Ananias and Saphira for lying to the Holy Spirit (Acts 5) to the less severe examples found in other pages of the New Testament, discipline sets an example for the rest of the Body and promotes godly fear (1 Timothy 5:20). The unintended consequence of unconcern in the face of the openly wicked is that other members of the congregation may note the lack of concern and be tempted to sin. "A little leaven leavens the whole lump" (1 Cor. 5:6).

So then, church discipline isn't exercised just for the benefit of the unrepentant, but is also to be carried out so that others within the congregation will take note and recognize that if they too fall into the same sentiment of sin and continue to live without repentance, they also will encounter the identical condemnation and judgment.

Indeed, it's a dreadful thought to consider that those whom we fail to warn may eventually be consigned to the fires of hell by God. Equally as frightful is the fact that unless we insist on the discipline of the openly wicked, God will take his wrath out on us! The Bible warns, "When I say to the wicked, 'You will surely die,' and you do not warn him or speak out to warn the wicked from his wicked way that he may live, that wicked man shall die in his iniquity, but his blood I will require at your hand" (Ezekiel 3:18).

Third, church discipline is intended to redeem the wayward soul. It's a fallacy that the admonition, censure, or barring of a member from the Lord's Table, or any other aspect of church life, is designed as a punishment. Don't interpret the distinction between formative and corrective church discipline to imply that the goal of corrective discipline is only to reprimand. It too has a positive purpose: the deliverance of the sinner. "Tough love" remedies are meant to get through to people where lesser measures have failed.

Discipline and love are not mutually exclusive. Discipline is an act of love. Returning to the incestuous brother at Corinth, Paul writes, "I have decided to deliver such a one to Satan for the destruction of his flesh, *so that his spirit may be saved in the day of the Lord Jesus*" (1 Corinthians 5:5, italics mine; see also 2 Thessalonians 3:6, James 5:19–20).

Yet we're not to rush to stern measures in attempting to bring people to their senses, but following the Lord's prescription, are to go to him in private, in prayer, and with great humility, lest in our conceit we commit the greater sin. Our Lord teaches, "If your brother sins, go and show him his fault in private; if he listens to you, you have won your brother. But if he does not listen to you, take one or two more with you, so that by the mouth of two or three witnesses every fact may be confirmed. If he refuses to listen to them, tell it to the church; and if he refuses to listen even to the church, let him be to you as a Gentile and a tax collector" (Matthew 18:15–17).

Discipline seeks healing: healing to the spirit trapped in sin, healing to the mind scarred by sin, and healing of relationships affected by sin. Consequently, the disciplinary process may be long, as it may take time for bonds of trust to be reattached and strengthened. Where sin has reared its ugly head, it harms relationships predicated on trust. It takes only a second for trust to be broken. But it may take a much longer time for it to be reestablished. Discipline under the auspices of the pastor and other leaders within the church helps to assure a successful outcome.

The Left Foot of Fellowship

What about excommunication? As the prophet warns, "The heart is more deceitful than all else and is desperately sick; who can understand it?" (Jeremiah 17:9). People aren't inclined to have ears to hear wise council, but are quick to defend themselves even in the face of overwhelming proof of their guilt. If a person should continue down this unwarranted path, excommunication becomes a real possibility.

Many church members question the use of excommunication, or what some churches call "disfellowshipping," believing it is never right. But to think this way is to substitute our reason for the Lord's infinite wisdom. If He says there comes a time when it's appropriate to treat the unrepentant as a Gentile, or a tax collector, then we must have faith in the Lord and in His understanding of the human condition. He's the Great Physician. No one knows with greater depth and detail the hardness of a man's heart, what it takes to break it, make it soft, and return it to seeking after the things of God. If Jesus says that excommunication is an option, then it's an option.

To avoid excommunication where it is warranted, thinking we are doing a person good, is actually to do him great harm. We're keeping him from the very medicine his sick and tired soul so desperately needs. Dietrick Bonhoeffer stated with great insight, "Nothing is so cruel as the tenderness that consigns another to his sin. Nothing can be more compassionate than the severe rebuke that calls a brother back from the path of sin."[1]

Though the world teaches that shaming a person is a moral crime, the Bible is clear that excommunication is intended to make the sinner feel shame. Paul writes, "If anyone does not obey our instruction in this letter, take special note of that person and do not associate with him, so that he will be put to shame" (2 Thessalonians 3:14). This shame is what causes sorrow, which in turn produces repentance. "For the sorrow that is according to the will of God produces a repentance without regret, leading to salvation, but the sorrow of the world produces death" (2 Corinthians 7:10).

Also important to note is that the excommunication of a member doesn't mean that this person is not a Christian. Christians are excommunicated. When a church court excommunicates a Christian, it is saying, "You may very well be a believer, but right now you are not acting like one, so this is how we are going to treat you." Also, I must stress once again that excommunication is an act of love. A church that excommunicates is saying, "We have tried everything to get you to turn from sin, but you refuse. This is the last tool in our arsenal we have to reach you. Please, please listen."

DEFINING "SUCCESSFUL OUTCOME"

As of this writing I've been in the ministry for about 25 years. In that time, I've witnessed many disciplinary cases within churches. It's been my observation that *most* people (at least those whose stories I have been able to keep up with) who fell under the auspices of discipline haven't yet repented of their sinful ways and sought reconciliation and restoration. That's an unfortunate commentary.

However, some people—praise God—have responded positively to corrective measures and are now functioning and ministering in good standing within their congregations. I can think of examples of elders,

---

1. Dietrich Bonhoeffer, *Life Together* (San Francisco: Harper, 1954), 107.

deacons, and laymen alike who, when caught in a pattern of sins and trespasses, heeded the call to return to the Lord.

Nonetheless, it's a heartbreaking fact that far too many people who claim to be Christians don't have "ears to hear" when lovingly and firmly confronted with their sin. I've heard it said that the fact of many failed cases of church discipline is reason enough to abandon the practice and move forward with the self-regulating, therapeutic managerial church model.

But what people who take this position neglect to see is that purported "failed" disciplinary cases remain open until the death of the offender. In some cases, it can take many years for the Spirit of God to work repentance into a reprobate's heart. As the old saying goes, "It ain't over till the fat lady sings." We must never surrender our prayers for the defiant soul.

What we should also ponder is the fact that even if a person should fail to respond positively to correction, this fact alone doesn't mean that the process failed. *Successful church discipline is the presence and function of church discipline. Unsuccessful church discipline is the absence of biblically prescribed church discipline.* It's rightly been said that the victory in evangelism is in the proclamation, not in how many people accept Jesus. The same applies to the area of church discipline. The ultimate victory in the practice of church discipline doesn't lie in how many people repent of their unbiblical behavior, but rests in the doing of it and the glory it brings to God in the process.

Another important way you can bring glory to God is through the use of your time and talents in the service of the kingdom of God. Join me as we explore this topic in the next chapter.

6

Why "The Consumer is Always Right" is Wrong

"Do what you can, with what you have, where you are."

—Theodore Roosevelt

CHRISTIAN SERVICE IS AT an all time low. It's my anecdotal observation that *most Christians spend 90 percent of their time on things that are of no eternal worth, while they give only about 10 percent of their time and energy to things that are of eternal value.* Their priorities are reflective of the narcissism of the age. Their lives are oriented toward making money and carving out a niche for themselves in the world. Little wonder there is not much "oomph" left in them when called upon to serve their local church. People attend worship services year after year. Many are even loyal, theologically orthodox, honorable people, but they lack the vitality, commitment to on-going discipleship, and courage to share their faith. They're rarely present in prayer meetings. One longs for a spark of God's Spirit to push them over the edge into the depths of a revived, holy zeal for Christ.

The comfortable Christian only ever wants to attend church and take in, but not give out. Such a person reminds me of a sponge that soaks in water but is never squeezed. One might guess what the sponge smells like after time. We can serve God with the strengths He has entrusted unto us and be a sweet smell in His nostrils. Or we can be like the bloated sponge. Let's take a cue from the life of Jesus, who said, "For even the Son of Man did not come to be served, but to serve, and to give His life a ransom for many." Since Jesus lives inside the believer, His mandate to serve God and others is the believer's mandate also. To shun the work of ministry is to shun the life of Christ within us.

Manipulating the Masses

Many pastors are well familiar with the struggle to encourage their people to take personal ownership of ministry. They continue to fight this uphill challenge. However, a new current is flowing within broad evangelicalism, in which shepherds of the flock, recognizing the extent to which the culture in the West has produced a consumer population, are now looking for ways to benefit from the situation (somewhat like I discussed in chapter 5 on church discipline). The trick is to minimize the pressure on church members and visitors alike to serve while placing the onus of responsibility for ministry on paid staff.

Not long ago, a woman shared with a close friend of mine her reason for attending a church. "Oh, we just love it there. They never ask us to do anything," she said. This church doesn't need to ask her to do anything because it's in a position to enlist paid professionals, including top-quality musicians, dancers, sound engineers, and actors, to do the work so the general congregation can sit back, relax, and soak it all in.

So it appears we have a problem being fed from both ends. On the one hand, scores of churchgoers are reticent to roll up their shirtsleeves and pitch in. In fact, not being asked to do anything actually makes a church attractive to some people. On the other hand, church leaders, seeing a golden opportunity to tap into this inclination, are careful to keep the accent off of service, hoping people will feel like an audience rather than participants. The snag is that even though these churches may maintain the façade of vigorous Christianity, and may also be growing numerically, they suffer from the same disease of apathy found in much smaller churches suffering stagnancy and decline.

CLOSE ENCOUNTERS OF THE 4TH KIND

What reason do people generally give for excusing themselves from active ministry? "We're just so busy right now." Ever heard that one? Let's focus on the operative word in this common response, the word "busy." There is an undertone associated with this word. The person who says they are too busy to serve wants you to react the same way as if he or she was abducted by aliens. Someone abducted by aliens is someone you can't reach. They're unavailable. It's not a matter of serving at a later time or calling me when things slow down. No, "I've been abducted by aliens," which means, "There's not now, nor will there ever be, a time when I am available."

But being busy is not like being abducted by aliens. While some of what keeps us busy represents things not in our control, most of what demands our time is the result of our own personal, lifestyle choices. Busyness is something that doesn't happen overnight. It's the result of a little decision here, a little decision there, that over the course of time accumulates and preoccupies our lives.

Hamster on a Treadmill

Our overly active lives are symptomatic of our failure to live under grace, so we always have to be working, doing. Yet, so little of our time is reserved for serving the Lord and laying up treasure in heaven. What's the number one thing that keeps us so busy? Stuff. What's stuff? It includes work, kids, school, shuttling the kids around, housework, sports, all of our personal projects, and more. Now, all of these things are important. For one, we must all work to make a living. "If anyone is not willing to work, then he is not to eat" (2 Thessalonians 3:10). We must also raise and care for our children.

Nevertheless, let me ask a question. "Are you controlling the stuff or is the stuff controlling you?" Does your life feel like an endless routine that's producing no eternal value? I'm not suggesting you relinquish your earthly responsibilities and live as a desert hermit. But permit me to offer a little advice by way of a question. What if you were to review the goals associated with your responsibilities in light of Christ's call to serve Him with your whole heart, mind, soul, and strength? This review may very well produce a redirection of your many responsibilities, which may then help you build the kingdom of God. For instance, perhaps you've recently returned to school to earn a degree. What is your motivation for doing so? To earn a better paycheck? To advance your career? To enhance your resume? Or do you see your degree, and potential career advancement, as a means to a larger end—a way to serve Jesus better? This is redirection.

Let's Be Honest

It's imperative that we lay our cards on the table and engage in a little self-confrontation. Openly and sincerely ask yourself, "Am I meeting my responsibility to be a laborer in God's vineyard?" *The temptation is always to be a very busy person, yet a very idle disciple.* How easy it is to take God's free grace for granted and yet not recognize that each of us are called to discharge a divinely-appointed purpose ordained by God before the foundations of the world. As His ambassadors, our commission is to work while it is day, to build His Church, to declare the glad hosannas of God in the midst of a crooked and perverse generation before time runs out. This is our privilege, our mission.

Procrastination?

We also must confess that too often we have placed the weighty things of God on hold, always promising to deal with them at a later time. "Tomorrow, tomorrow, I will do it," we say. But tomorrow never comes. Who are we to adjourn the business of the King's court when the King Himself yet presides over heaven and earth? What right do we have to postpone the King's affairs when no such order has been received from heaven? The fleeting things and pleasures of the world, the lesser loyalty, so easily entangle us in the Christian race; they absorb our fascination, robbing us of our fervor for Christ, service to His kingdom, and our passion to win souls for Jesus.

The Cultural Impact

To this point, I've mentioned a few times how our churches are prone to let the culture dictate how ministry is to be carried out. Yet here's an example from early church history of how one Christian's service both within and outside the strictures of the churches had a profound effect on the shape of public policy.

In a letter of 362 addressed to Arsacius, high priest of Galatia, Emperor Julian the Apostate (r. 361–363 A.D.), an ardent defender of the canonized gods of Rome, was stunned that the Christian mission continued to thrive even after the state-approved religious ceremonies had been restored. Julian could only demand that the priests in Galatia follow the example of the Christians by incorporating their beliefs into a positive social program. "Why then do we think that this is sufficient and do not observe how the kindness of Christians to strangers, their care for the burial of their dead, and the sobriety of their lifestyle has done the most to advance their cause? Each of these things, I think, ought really to be practiced by us."[1]

He then proceeded to decree a series of prohibited actions. No priest was to be seen in a bar, visit the theatre, or engage in improper talk. Julian then commanded that Arsacius set up a system of hostels in every city in Galatia for the purpose of charity. "Furthermore, 1/5 of 30,000 modii of wheat and 60,000 pints of wine allocated to Galatia were to be used for charity distribution. Julian told Arsacius that the helping of the community by the priests was the way of the forefathers, with such practices dating to the time of Homer."[2] We can have the same remarkable impact on the surrounding culture, if only we're willing.

SOME STRONG MEDICINE

Sleepy-headed believers are generally repulsed by strong directives designed to stir them to love and good deeds. But in Matthew 25, Jesus uses allegory and rich symbolism, looking at us with razors in His eyes, ready to teach us about the danger of spiritual laziness.

Here Jesus tells the allegory of a businessman, who before embarking on a trip entrusts his money to his servants to develop while he's away. To one man he gave five talents, to another two talents, and to yet another one talent. Alas, the guy given the one talent, out of fear that something might happen to it, buried it so it wouldn't be lost. When his Master returned home, he severely judged this man for his unadventurous attitude. The servant was good not to lose the one talent, but neither did he develop it. Consequently, he was judged in such a way as if he had lost it. "Throw out the worthless slave into the outer darkness; in that place there shall be weeping and gnashing of teeth" (v. 30)

Many of us are not much different from the guy with the one talent. Perhaps you're not living in flagrant sin, so at least on that level you're ready for Jesus to return. But what are you doing *positively* for Christ by way of developing the gifts He's entrusted to you? *Being ready for Christ's return means more than not being caught doing bad deeds. It also means being found doing good deeds.*

---

1. Walter Robert, "Julian the Apostate (360–363 A.D.)" http://www.roman-emperors .org/julian.htm.

2. Ibid.

A Stunning Moral Equivalent

Take one more look at Matthew 25:26. The Master calls his faithless servant a "wicked, lazy slave." Notice the association between laziness and wickedness. Now if I were to poll an evangelical congregation and ask, "How many lazy bones failed to take out the garbage on time," a lot of hands would go up. But if asked, "How many wicked, immoral, iniquitous pagans do we have here?" I suspect very few hands would be raised. My point is that society has minimized the true meaning of laziness. This attitude has greatly influenced the churches. Laziness is not merely the lack of energy to accomplish a task. It's also the presence of iniquity in the heart, which reveals itself as sloth and indolence. So let me ask once more. Are you using your gifts and talents in the service of the King of Kings? Or are you playing it safe?

BUILDING THE KINGDOM OF GOD

The Bible goes to great lengths to encourage us to use our lives in the service of His Church. Using figures of speech, Ephesians 5:23 and Colossians 1:18 refer to Christ as the "head" and the church as His "body." 1 Corinthians 12 further explains how the Church is made up of individuals who work together, pooling their talents, skills, and strengths—all for the purpose of helping as many people grow in their relationship with God. The Lord also calls us to share our faith. Matthew 28:18–20 records the Lord's Great Commission, in which each believer is commanded to be an active personal evangelist, sharing the gospel of salvation with those in need of God's forgiveness.

The Cornerstone

Using other rich symbolism, the Bible equates the Church to a building. Like any building, it has a foundation. Christ is the foundation. Elsewhere, Jesus is called the "cornerstone" of the Church (Luke 20:17). Paul says of himself that he is a "wise master builder" that laid the foundation, who is "Christ, and Him crucified" (1 Cor. 3:10, also 2:2). It's upon this foundation, Paul goes on to say, that everything within the Church is to be built. Paul was not the only builder. All members of the Body of Christ, he says, are to help build the Church.

Also, we are not to build the Church any way we see fit, but are to be *careful* how we build (v.10). There are some who build properly:

they build with gold, silver, and precious stones. These are things that symbolize work in keeping with the holy nature of the foundation (v.12). But there are others who are not so careful how they build. They build with wood, hay, and straw, things that are not in keeping with the holy nature of the foundation (v. 12). Someday both groups will have their work tested as by fire. To the one whose life's service is of the nature of gold, silver, and precious stones, the fire will not harm it. In fact, the fire will reveal its precious qualities. But to the one whose life's work is of the nature of wood, hay, and straw, the fire will burn it up (vss. 13–15).

Even with these clear biblical teachings before us, so few people are willing to roll up their shirtsleeves, pitch in, and minister. I've seen it all: poor attendance in Sunday school, how terribly hard it is to get volunteers, people taking their seats after the first hymn has started, people attending church services for months, and even years, but never getting involved in active ministry. Oh yes, they come to church. But somehow they always seem to manage to keep the church at arm's length. They get close to the church, but not *too* close. I see these recurrent patterns of sluggishness and can't help but wonder, "Are these people being careful builders?" The Lord has this to say to those who treat the Christian life like a casual walk in the park. "Woe to those who are at ease in Zion and to those who feel secure in the mountain of Samaria" (Amos 6:1).

ONE LIFE TO LIVE FOR CHRIST

What will be your legacy? Do you understand that you get *one shot* at the Christian life? When the tail of the tape is read and your work for Christ is revealed, there's no doctoring the results. It is what it is. You say, "I'm not sure I can do all that much to serve Christ."

Here's some advice on how you can become a better servant of God.

The person who thinks he can do only a little for the Lord and for His Church must understand that being a careful builder means to build with quality not quantity. 1 Corinthians 3:13 states that each man's work will be "revealed with fire, and the fire itself will test the *quality* of each man's work" (emphasis mine). So it's the quality, not the quantity of our labor for God that really matters. Nevertheless, in the church of today, quality has taken a back seat to quantity. The goal of most evangelical churches is to be "a mile wide and an inch deep."

Not long ago, I attended a conference for pastors, and each time I introduced myself to another pastor, I was asked, "How big is your church?" No one ever asked about the church's spiritual depth. That God is going to test the *quality* of each man's work means that the size of our ministry or church is secondary. Applied to laymen, this means that one's contribution to the Church need not be big. Rather, it should be an expression of one's relationship with Christ.

Quality service is also service that is done well. One of the other patterns I've witnessed over the years is the Sunday school teacher or ministry leader showing up unprepared, hoping to "wing it." In Old Testament verbiage this leader is bringing a blemished sacrifice into the house of the Lord, and God does not approve. You don't need to be an expert in the Bible, have a Doctor of Education degree to teach Sunday school, or have years of experience in an area of ministry to do ministry well. Simply judge your gifts rightly and seek a place of service where those gifts can be used. Begin slowly, but thoughtfully, prepare your plan carefully, and bathe it in prayer. God will use you and you will discover the blessing of being an able and careful builder of the Kingdom of God.

Whatever you do, don't be intimidated by those who do a lot for the Lord. Many of us look at people doing great things for God and naturally assume they're people of much greater talent, whom we could never match, so we throw ours hands in the air. But how do you know that the person you admire is not just an average person, much like you, who made himself available to God, and God used him mightily? There are people with less talent doing more with the little they have than those with great talent who are doing next to nothing. *Don't overlook the little differences you can make today because you're caught up trying to make a big difference in the light of a tomorrow you can't guarantee.*

The good works God calls us to do for Him are His work done through us. Let's not ever think that Christian service is the result of human effort. Hosea says, "From Me comes your fruit" (Hosea 14:8, see also John 15:5). The prophet's words remind us that every good work is a prize of our precious union with Christ. Like the fruit of the tree that was first in the stem, so all our good works were first in Christ and then brought forth in us. Our mistake is to understand what God has called us to perform to His glory, but then try to *make* it happen. But fruit isn't forced, as if in an artificial way. It's always yielded by the Vine.

Paul even tells *when* God determined our works. He says, "For we are His workmanship, created in Christ Jesus for good works, which God prepared beforehand so that we would walk in them" (Ephesians 2:10). Here's an amazing and freeing truth. It means that even before the earth was created, God had already determined the nature and the scope of our labor for Him. Some people fear they've done too little for Him. While others look at what God has called them to do, and fear it's too much. But that God arranged our good works before the foundations of the world, and that He's the Vine and we're the branches, means that God established both the extent, and the source, of our fruitfulness in this life.

THE SALT OF THE EARTH

A final word of encouragement for those who don't think they have anything to offer is found in the words of our Lord. He said, "You are the salt of the earth" (Matthew 5:13). Then He said, "You are the light of the world" (v. 14). Notice that Jesus didn't tell His disciples, "You *can* be the salt of the earth." He said, "You *are* the salt of the earth." Once more, He didn't say, "You *can* be the light of the world." He said, "You *are* the light of the world." As a disciple of Jesus, you don't need to aspire to be salt and light. You *are* salt and light. Right now you're an illuminating and preserving influence for Christ. You just need to get off the shelf of busyness, procrastination, and lethargy and be in practice what God has already made you to be in principle.

The process begins with letting your knees hit the floor, crying out to Him, repenting of any laziness, excuses, and double-mindedness. Ask Him to fill you with His Spirit. He'll use you in ways you never thought possible! God will likely start you off slow. But He'll make a way.

Christian service inevitably entails opposition and hardship. If you're prepared to suffer for Christ, caution! You're about to be really challenged.

7

The Missing Mark of Authentic Christianity

*"The greater our sufferings the more closely
do we conform to our baptism."*

—MARTIN LUTHER

*"Be of good comfort, Master Ridley, and play the man. We shall this day
light such a candle, by God's grace in England, as I trust shall never be
put out."*

—HUGH LATIMER TO NICHOLAS RIDLEY
UPON THEIR DEATHS AT THE STAKE

NEAR THE END OF Homer's *The Odyssey*, we read about Odysseus finally returning home after years of wandering. Because he's disguised as an old man, no one recognizes him, not even his family. That night, just before bed, Eurycleia, the aged nurse of Odysseus, bathes him—thinking she is bathing an old visitor for the night. While scrubbing him, she notices a scar on Odysseus' leg and immediately recognizes it as the same scar she saw when he was an infant. It was then that she recognized Odysseus.

According to John 20:19–23, the disciples didn't recognize their risen Lord until they saw His scars. But in distinction from Homer's story, the biblical account raises perplexing questions. Why does the risen Christ even have scars? Are we not to receive glorified bodies without blemish, and is not Jesus' glorified body the very model of such a new body? Why would Jesus' glorified body retain any reminders of His suffering?

Jesus' scars are evidence of His authenticity. They distinguish Him from the gods of all false religions who do not have wounds. They're all perfect. Examine the depictions of Aton-Ra of Egypt, the snake goddess of Minoan religion, the Classical gods and goddesses of early Greece and Rome, Shiva Vishnu of the Hindu religion, Buddha, Krishna, and many more. You'll see no marks on their bodies. They're flawless. They're perfect in body because they never suffered for our sins. The mark of Jesus' authenticity is not His smooth, unblemished, resurrected flesh, but the scar tissue of His glorified body. Jesus' scars are, above all things, the unique marks of the Redeemer.

Are You Genuine?

An important mark of the Christian's authenticity is also found in his scars. Peter instructs us, "Therefore, since Christ has suffered in the flesh, arm yourselves also with the same purpose, because he who has suffered in the flesh has ceased from sin" (1 Peter 4:1). And Paul says, "For to you it has been granted for Christ's sake, not only to believe in Him, but also to suffer for His sake, experiencing the same conflict, which you saw in me, and now hear to be in me" (Philippians 1:29–30). Are you willing to suffer for Christ? Do you bear the scars of that suffering? Are you an authentic Christian?

To attempt to embrace the benefits of His resurrection without the sufferings associated with His cross produces in our lives the veneer of Christianity without the substance. Becoming a Christian doesn't mean the end of suffering. It's all the more reason you will suffer. Your friends and family may disown you, co-workers may marginalize you, and the world may persecute you even to the point of death. Dare we forget that our sufferings for Christ are, as the Apostle Paul says, "granted" to us? The sufferings we undergo for Him are not mistakes, sad accidents, or terrible twists of fate. They are blessings. We know they are blessings because He has granted them unto us. The very idea of God bequeathing to us a thing means it is intended to bless us and to glorify Him. Embrace His sufferings. The flesh will resist. But remember, *the spirit of a man will only count as loss what the flesh at first counts as gain, and the same spirit will only count as gain what the flesh at first counts as loss*

PACIFICATION NOT PERSECUTION

As a rule, we evangelicals have forgotten to suffer for Christ. We've abandoned the offense of the gospel. Let me ask a pointed question. When will the American church produce a martyr? I'm not asking when a missionary from the U.S. will die as a martyr in China or in a Muslim country. I'm asking, "When are we going to see a martyr for Christ *in* America?"[1] The very question should cause the reader to pause and reflect upon the evangelical mentality that doesn't even think in these terms. Do you see anything in the new direction broad evangelicalism is taking which would provide a lively context for the open persecution of believers? If anything, we're going out of our way to accommodate ourselves to the culture. The modern gospel, a bequeath of the secular culture, is expressed mainly in terms of victory, power, triumph, and success—those expressions of faith that leave no room for persecution.

In its glorious eleventh chapter, the Book of Hebrews places the privilege of martyrdom in the context of faith. As in the case of Abraham, faith articulates a willingness to sacrifice anything God requires (v. 17), even one's own life (vss. 36–37). During New Testament times, the gospel so transformed believers that they were willing to march into hell and kick Satan in the knees. These people were sold out to the gospel, willing to die for it. They made such an impact on their culture that they were charged with "upset[ting] the world" (Acts 17:6). Today the exact opposite is the case. The last thing we want to do, it seems, is upset the world. The new strategy is to placate the world. It is a strategy of appeasement. So we've offered concessions.

The Silent Bible?

How do we read passages from the Bible that deal with persecution when there's absolutely nothing in our lives for which we could be persecuted? Consider this example from 1 Peter.

---

1. We have at least one example in modern times. On April 20, 1999, Cassie Bernall, a junior at Columbine High in Littleton, Colorado, was a typical teenager experiencing a typical day when Dylan Harris and Eric Klebold walked into school and began to open fire. Entering the library, Harris soon trained a gun on Cassie and asked if she believed in God. She said "Yes." The killer then shot Cassie in the head, killing her instantly. Some reports claim that the exchange actually happened between Klebold and surviving student Valeen Schnurr.

> Beloved, do not be surprised at the fiery ordeal among you, which comes upon you for your testing, as though some strange thing were happening to you; but to the degree that you share the sufferings of Christ, keep on rejoicing, so that also at the revelation of His glory you may rejoice with exultation. If you are reviled for the name of Christ, you are blessed, because the Spirit of glory and of God rests on you. Make sure that none of you suffers as a murderer, or thief, or evildoer, or a troublesome meddler; but if anyone suffers as a Christian, he is not to be ashamed, but is to glorify God in this name. For it is time for judgment to begin with the household of God; and if it begins with us first, what will be the outcome for those who do not obey the gospel of God? And if it is with difficulty that the righteous is saved, what will become of the godless man and the sinner? Therefore, those also who suffer according to the will of God shall entrust their souls to a faithful Creator in doing what is right (1 Peter 4:12–19).

Peter is writing to a group of believers scattered on the outskirts of Asia Minor who are about to be brutally persecuted by the deranged Emperor Nero. He offers them unwavering hope in Christ, reasons for their testing, and council regarding how they ought to live in the face of death. Now, there's no doubt that the sufferings of Christ include a variety of trials beside persecution. God can use any problem you face, whether it is physical, financial, or relational, as a context for your spiritual growth. Nonetheless, the sufferings of Christ have first and foremost to do with persecution. Peter says, "if anyone suffers *as a Christian*" (1 Peter 4:16, italics mine) to distinguish the pains and anguish Christians share with unbelievers as a result of our common heritage in Adam from the suffering that is conjoined to the Christian witness, which is persecution. Could it be that our dishonor is that the *only* things we can apply 1 Peter to is everything BUT persecution?

Here are just a few more examples of biblical texts that speak of suffering for the cause of the gospel in a fallen world.

> "Remember the word that I said to you, 'A slave is not greater than his master.' If they persecuted Me, they will also persecute you" (John 15:20).

> In this you greatly rejoice, even though now for a little while, if necessary, you have been distressed by various trials, so that the proof of your faith, being more precious than gold which is perishable, even though tested by fire, may be found to result in

praise and glory and honor at the revelation of Jesus Christ (1 Peter 1:6–7).

And He summoned the crowd with His disciples, and said to them, "If anyone wishes to come after Me, he must deny himself, and take up his cross and follow Me. For whoever wishes to save his life will lose it, but whoever loses his life for My sake and the gospel's will save it. For what does it profit a man to gain the whole world, and forfeit his soul? For what will a man give in exchange for his soul? For whoever is ashamed of Me and My words in this adulterous and sinful generation, the Son of Man will also be ashamed of him when He comes in the glory of His Father with the holy angels" (Mark 8:34–38).

Do these passages apply to your life? In what way has your testimony created a refiner's fire in which your faith is being tested as gold? How has your Christian testimony brought you close to sacrificing your body? Oh, trust me, I include myself in these hard questions. So, what are our answers? Are we to rip these teachings out of the Bible? What does it mean that large sections of the New Testament have become totally obsolete to an entire generation of Christians? The Word of God has not changed. We have. We're only able to apply these passages to the problems we share with the world as a result of our common heritage in Adam because far too many of us are not living the real deal.

Outside of countries where persecution is a living reality, we Protestant evangelicals in the West have no valid experience of Christian suffering because we do nothing to stir the enemy. The great lie of Satan is that of the conventional god. And far too many of us have accepted it, pep-talks, saunas, and all. Perhaps if our conventionalized churches get the message and open their doors to the power of Christ, we can get back to basics, stir the enemy, and live the real deal.

OUR OWN WORST ENEMY?

The evangelical movement is no longer a threat to the world system. Secular forces may contest the Christian faith and the Western culture that was founded on the Judeo-Christian ethic, but we in the contemporary evangelical church have so trivialized Christianity that we're no longer considered worthy of opposition. How can we be taken seriously when the best we can offer are TV hosts sitting around the potted plants fawning over cheesy Christian culture; self-proclaimed Bishops without a diocese preaching the bizarre, the heretical, and the fruity; and books which, due to their intellectual vacuity and self-absorbed narcissism, are nothing more than ultra-long Hallmark cards? Where's the bonfire of the vanities when you really need it?

Pigeon-holing the Stuff We Don't Like

One glaring reason we're no longer a threat to the world system is due to our propensity to compartmentalize the "words in red." Jesus said, "If anyone comes to Me, and does not hate his own father and mother and wife and children and brothers and sisters, yes, and even his own life, he cannot be My disciple. Whoever does not carry his own cross and come after Me cannot be My disciple" (Luke 14:26–27). Elsewhere He said, "No one can serve two masters; for either he will hate the one and love the other, or he will be devoted to one and despise the other. You cannot serve God and wealth" (Matthew 6:24).

These adages are part of a special little group of sayings that we've conveniently quarantined under "the hard sayings of Jesus." The category is like a chest of old stuff you don't want to throw away but don't wish to keep in the living room for everyone to see, so you stuff all of it in the attic. However, the Bible doesn't speak of the hard sayings of Jesus. His call to be willing and ready to endure persecution for His name's sake is simply the way the Master defined discipleship. If what He said is hard, it's only so because it's hard for us to hear.

Exposed!

Let me come clean. Do you want to know a little secret? The fact is, when it comes to shunning Christian persecution, there's never been a greater offender than me. I can even recall the exact day. My first year as a seminarian, I decided to take a course in evangelism. I showed up for the first class, which, to my surprise, didn't meet at the school but in downtown Philadelphia. We were actually going to do evangelism! "Well," I ruminated silently, "I'm not exactly sure I'm ready for this." Then it happened. The class instructor informed us that we were going into the streets to do one-on-one evangelism. "Woe, wait a minute," I thought to myself. So as we all marched down the street to the main intersection where there were lots of people, I made sure to remain in the back of the line.

Once we arrived at our destination, our teacher instructed us to strike up some conversations with people and see if we couldn't bridge into a discussion on salvation. I stood by and watched. Seeing that I wasn't engaging anyone in conversation, our teacher walked over, grabbed me by the arm, and escorted me to a young, Hispanic boy. He then asked the young man his name. "My name's Enrique," he replied. The professor then looked at me and said, "John, Enrique. Enrique, John. John go!"

I knew what he meant. He was directing me to share the gospel with young Enrique. After a few minutes of fumbling my way through an atrocious presentation of the gospel, the teacher stepped in and gave him a crystal clear presentation of the good news of salvation by grace through faith in Christ.

After class, I returned to my rented room, laid on my bed, and began to cry. I felt mortified. In that moment it hit me why I had been so reluctant to speak to people earlier that day about the gospel. I really didn't care about them, including Enrique. What's more, I was in fear of what others might think of me. I didn't want to appear as a fool before people. It was then that I realized that the whole episode had exposed me as a fake. Right then and there, lying on that bed, I said something to God I'll never forget. I prayed, "God, make me real or get me out."

I didn't want to be a "professional" minister. Somehow I just knew that unless I had a heart for the lost and was willing to be counted a fool for Christ, to suffer persecution for His name, I shouldn't be in the ministry. God did a wonderful thing that afternoon. He changed me. He gave me a heart for the lost and courage to overcome the fear of human opinion.

It's my heartfelt prayer for all of us suffering the illusion of loving the lost, when in fact we have no intention to speak to anyone about their need for Christ, that we too would be willing to say to God, "Make me real."

JOY IN PERSECUTION

What may assist us in rediscovering the missing mark of authentic Christianity in our lives is the fact that nowhere else is the experience of true joy more complete than in our shared experience of Christ's sufferings. Luke records the great joy Paul and his missionary companions experienced as they bore affliction for the Name above all names. He writes, "So they went on their way from the presence of the Council, rejoicing that they had been considered worthy to suffer shame for His name" (Acts 5:41, see also 9:16).

Paul is so full of joy in his experience of hardship and possible death in the service of Christ that he treats it as "momentary, light affliction" (2

Corinthians 4:17) compared "with the glory that is to be revealed to us" (Romans 8:18). Peter encourages us not to lose our joyful hope in enduring difficulty as a Christian, for bearing up under such adversity serves to please God (1 Peter 2:10), beget blessing (3:14; 4:14), and glorify the Father (4:16).

In Philippians, known as the "Epistle of Joy," Paul sets the joy of Christian living in the context of Christian maltreatment. He says that one of his greatest desires is "that I may know Him and the power of His resurrection and the fellowship of His sufferings, being conformed to His death" (Philippians 3:10). Note the close association between "the power of His resurrection" and "the fellowship of His sufferings." A lot of people are desirous of the power of Christ, but not His sufferings. But the wedding of these two concepts teaches us that unless we join with Jesus in the fellowship of His sufferings, we shall not know the power of His resurrection. No suffering, no power!

But the more important point I wish to make is this: notice once more the phrase "and the fellowship of His sufferings." This is where sweet fellowship with Christ is found, not in ecstatic spiritual experiences, gatherings designed to enflame enthusiasm, or in books promising a better, stress-reducing spirituality, but in the bond of His sufferings. We experience His fellowship in the worship of Him and also in our celebration of His Table. But never forget that when we fellowship with Him in His sufferings, there is also abundant joy.

Beloved reader, are you missing out on the joy of knowing Christ? Forsake not His sufferings!

Finish the Race

Perhaps you're one for whom suffering great travail for the cause of Christianity is not new. Do not lose heart in doing what is good. To encourage us to persevere in sacrificial living, the writer of Hebrews elicits the terminology of the Greek games "and let us run with endurance the race that is set before us" (12:1). Eusebius also uses this central device in his *Historia Ecclesiastica*, in which he refers to Christian martyrs as "athletes of God."[2] Paul uses similar terminology in his encouragement to the Church at Corinth to "run in such a way that you may win" (1 Corinthians 9:24).

2. See HE, VI.1.

THE "WHY" OF PERSECUTION: EVANGELISM

Why does Christ call us to suffer if He already suffered for us? Paul has the answer. He writes, "Now I rejoice in my sufferings for your sake, and in my flesh I do my share on behalf of His body, which is the church, in filling up what is lacking in Christ's afflictions" (Colossians 1:24). Paul isn't saying that Jesus' sufferings on the cross were somehow inadequate to fully atone for our sins and that his suffering finishes the task. The pain and anguish Jesus endured for His people on the cross paid the price of their redemption in full. Paul is not talking about suffering related to the *propitiation* for sins, but to suffering associated with the *proclamation* of the gospel. In making Christ known to a fallen world, our afflictions *fill out* the afflictions of Jesus.

With this thought in mind, consider all those saints who came before you whose sacrifice helped make it possible for you to hear or to read the gospel and to be saved. Have you ever wondered how many prayers, tears, heartaches, disappointments, and deaths for the sake of the gospel people underwent leading to your conversion? Read the Scriptures and the testimony of history and see how much it cost the blood of the martyrs and the tears of persecuted people down through the centuries to keep the gospel fire burning. See the sweat and labor of translators and the effort of teachers so that we could have the Bible in our hands. Never take it for granted. Remember that someone suffered to make it possible.

But you too, dear reader, are also called to be a link in the chain of suffering leading to the new birth of someone else. Paul does not merely speak for himself. He is an example unto us. This is why he can say confidently that just as he has been called upon to fill up Christ's afflictions, so also God has granted unto us to suffer, to experience the same conflict the Apostle underwent himself (Philippians 1:29). Paul recounts some of his conflict. Oh the suffering! "Dangers from rivers, dangers from robbers, dangers from my countrymen, dangers from the Gentiles, dangers in the city, dangers in the wilderness, dangers on the sea, dangers among false brethren" (2 Corinthians 11:26).

Which words reappears over and again? "Dangers!" *The Christian life is a dangerous life.* Are you a dangerous Christian? Are you a threat to the world? Read the whole of 2 Corinthians 11:23–33. He was beaten with rods, shipwrecked, went without food and drink, and lived in unbearable conditions without proper shelter. How does your list of afflictions for the propagation of the gospel compare to Paul's. Mine pales in comparison. But if God calls us to experience the *same* conflict Paul underwent to evangelize the world (and this is what the Bible says!), what does this say about our need to get busy with biblical evangelism? And to do so shamelessly, boldly, uncompromisingly, and without fear of what man can do to us?

VICTORY IN JESUS

Only until evangelical Protestantism once again gladly bears a cross for Christ, while at the same time wielding the sword of the Spirit in evangelism, will the world take notice and will there be real change in our contiguous culture.

Here's a beautiful example taken from the pages of ancient church history of how Christians suffered for their testimony and how that testimony shook the world to its foundations.

During ancient Roman times, literally scores of believers were arrested on account of their witness. As they faced trial and eventual death, hardly anyone failed to take note of the radiant joy on their faces. While in the throes of death, they sang hymns of praise and continued to herald "Jesus is Lord" until they no longer had the breath to do so. That the Christian witness continued to the very end of the excruciating process of physical death stood as a towering testimony to the veracity of the gospel and acted as a magnet drawing in many unbelievers and hecklers to the ranks of the Church. Tertullian had noted that in this period, perhaps more than in any other, "the blood of martyrs was the seed of the Church."[3] Lions, beheadings, flaying, and being run through with the sword—nothing could remove the song from the Christians' lips. In time, not only did the pagan world lose the stomach to kill, but also many persecutors were so moved by the unshakable courage of believers facing death that they themselves became believers. The Church overcame evil with good.

This is how we shall overcome evil in our day: by living the gospel, proclaiming the gospel, and wearing the mark of authentic Christianity—that of suffering for the gospel—and doing so with great joy.

To this point, I have analyzed but a partial list of relevant issues pertaining to evangelical church-life. But what's the common denominator that makes these problems, problems?

---

3. *Apology*, L.14. Actually he said, "The blood of Christians is seed."

8

Would You Like Your Religion Puréed, Grated, or Mixed?

"Be not conformed to this world."

—Paul the Apostle

Today much of the evangelical church crafts belief, worships God, and evangelizes the world using the world's value system. Even a casual glance of our churches shows our propensity for taking the Bible and the trends of the culture, throwing them into the blender, and calling the result Christian. It's everywhere: from the ease with which we appear to accept the winds of doctrine without discernment, to entertainment-driven worship services, to fashionable sermons that hold the Bible in one hand and *People Magazine* in the other, to providing Santa Claus the same stage as the Lord Jesus during Christmas celebrations. This amalgamation of God with culture is producing scores of churches that are full of thousands, in some cases tens-of-thousands, of people. But most of them experience only nominal belief at best.

The Biblical Warning

The temptation to blend the teachings of God with the fallen trends of culture was a problem of paramount significance in the life of the ancient Jews. Daniel 9 records the day Daniel rediscovered the writings of Jeremiah. In his study of these important writings, Daniel could see that the 70 years of Jewish captivity were coming to a close. But what had the Jewish people done to deserve such a terrible punishment?

The Bible reveals that Israel had practiced a very dangerous form of false worship called Baalism. In ancient times, Baal was considered the god of weather, who blessed fertility, both human and agricultural. Such fruitfulness was thought to be encouraged by worshipping Baal through erotic sexual practices. But there's a sense in which we can speak of Baalism in even broader terms than fertility rites. It was a form of religion that embraced whatever was popular in the culture at the time.

Moreover, ancient Israel never worshipped Baal to the exclusion of the worship of God. Rather, she took the elements of popular culture and *intertwined* them with the Law of Moses and created a synthesis. So then, Israel's embrace of Baal can really be compared to the likes of America Atheists, an organization that flatly denies the existence of a personal God. By fusing God with the popular trends of the culture, the Old Testament Jews attempted to have the best of both worlds. They used godless culture as a vehicle for religious experience. The great prophet Elijah addressed this religious syncretism head-on when he declared to the people, "How long will you hesitate between two opinions? If the LORD is God, follow Him; but if Baal, follow him" (1 Kings 18:21).

Still Don't Get It?

We find an analogous admonition in the teachings of Jesus. In His comments on leaven (yeast), Jesus warned His disciples, "Watch out! Beware of the leaven of the Pharisees and the leaven of Herod" (Mark 8:15). Leaven symbolizes human imperfection. The Pharisees were the religious traditionalist of their day. They were conservative insofar as they believed in the supernatural, angels, spirits, a personal God, the Scriptures as the Word of God, and the resurrection of the dead. They erred inasmuch as they added to the Word of God traditions, thoughts, ideals, rituals, and ceremonies not contained in the Word of God. The result was that they placed big burdens on people that they couldn't bear. They were also very self-righteous, believing that a person gets to heaven through good works.

The Sadducees, or Herodians, were the opposite of the Pharisees. They were the theological and political liberals of their day. Theologically, they didn't believe in angels, spirits, the resurrection of the body, or the whole of the Old Testament (although they did believe the first five books, the Torah, to be scriptural). Politically, they held that big government would save the day. They were sympathetic with Herod, believing that through him the kingdom of heaven would come.

Now put the two together and what do you have? The fallen world system. For in the Pharisees and the Sadducees is represented the extremes of all that denies the Bible as the Word of God. Thus, Jesus' comment on leaven repeats the Old Testament warning about Baal and not mixing the elements of the fallen culture with the teachings of the Scriptures. That both testaments alert us to this hazard underscores how easily the elements of the contiguous culture seem unavoidably to work their way into, and become part of, the life of any church community to such an extent that it is possible to be a Christian and live within a pagan value system and not even recognize it.

We Dare Not Slacken Off

The Dust Bowl of the 1930s witnessed a period of severe dust storms, mainly across America's Great Plain. Dust clouds, sometimes reaching heights of 60 feet or more, were known to barrel across the open plains at speeds as high as 40 to, on rare occasions, 100 miles an hour! Once these storms hit the poorly-constructed, wood-slated farm houses, dust entered through the cracks of the walls and covered everything in the homes. Mothers would sweep and sweep but could never eliminate all the dust piling up on the floors. People lived in such unbearable conditions of dust that before they ate they kept their plates turned upside down on the table until the food was served. They would then turn their plates face up and gobble it down just as fast as they could before the food itself was covered with dust.

Now imagine how small a particle of dust is and then think about how easily it entered through the cracks of those old wooden homes. Leaven is even smaller than a speck of dust. My point is how easy the leaven of unbelief can find its way into your Christian experience should there be just the slightest crack in your spiritual armor. Once it enters your life it can contaminate your whole body, mind, and soul. Now you see why Jesus is so adamant in His warning to us to guard against allowing the patterns of the fallen, pagan culture access to the Church. They enter so easily and do great damage.

The ease with which pagan values work their way into the mission of the Church, contaminating everything in sight, means it's simply not enough to worship and to evangelize. We must be diligent to carry out the mission of the Church *according to the Word of God.* Unless God's Word remains central to all that we do and think, the Church will embrace the world's ways and forget God's. Frankly, this has already been happening on a grand scale.

THE PATH OF LEAST RESISTANCE

How have the elements of the popular culture blended so effortlessly with established, biblical theology and practice? Through what I call "sound-right theology." Sound-right theology encourages us to accept something as truth simply because it sounds right. It doesn't matter if it *is* right, it just needs to sound right. No need for further study or discernment in the light of the Bible to determine whether or not it is actually true. If it sounds right, that's good enough.

Have you noticed that although many believers carry Bibles to church, much of what they believe is based in their *feelings*, which are conditioned by the trends of the broader culture? Incorporating fleeting feelings and culture-driven trends into our reflection on what we ought to believe and how we ought to act is dangerous and repeats the basic sin for which ancient Israel was punished when she followed after Baal.

Interestingly, once weighed on the scales of Scripture, a lot of stuff that sounds right *isn't* right. Here are just a few examples of sound-right theology weighed against what the Bible actually says.

Sound-Right Theology Put to the Test

How many times have you heard that the big problem with kids today is that they suffer from poor self-esteem? Causes can include physical features, lack of education, emotional abuse by a parent, self-loathing, and more. When you heard this, didn't it sound right? And yet, this is not what Jesus taught. He inferred that the real problem with kids today and with people in general isn't that their self-esteem is too low, but that it's too high. He said, "If anyone wishes to come after Me, he must deny himself, and take up his cross and follow Me" (Mark 8:34).

Here's another example of sound-right theology. It's called "the age of accountability." This is the idea that God doesn't hold young children accountable for their sin until they are old enough to comprehend its consequences. Now most certainly this position sounds like it must be right. Not at all. The age of accountability is not found anywhere in the Bible. It is the fruit of the modern psychology movement, which also has given us the "insanity defense."

Remove the leaven of modern psychology and what does the Bible actually say regarding a young child's accountability before a Holy God?

> There is none righteous, not even one; there is none who understands, there is none who seeks for God; all have turned aside, together they have become useless; there is none who does good, there is not even one. Their throat is an open grave, with their tongues they keep deceiving, the poison of asps is under their lips; whose mouth is full of cursing and bitterness; their feet are swift to shed blood, destruction and misery are in their paths, and the path of peace they have not known. There is no fear of God before their eyes (Romans 3:10–18).

Do you read any "clauses" in Paul's quote that exempt young kids from the consequences of sin? I don't. In fact, Paul sums up the human condition in these stark terms, "for *all* have sinned and fall short of the glory of God" (v. 23, italics mine). Who does "all" include? All. Everyone. Every person, from the youngest to the oldest, has sinned against God and is therefore responsible for their sinful nature and their actual sins. What is sin's biggest consequence? "For the wages of sin is death" (6:23a).[1] But praise be to God that "the free gift of God is eternal life in Christ Jesus our Lord" (v.23b).

The Right Not to Be Offended

A few years ago my wife, Bonnie, had an experience with sound-right theology. She decided to attend a Bible study at a local church because she had heard that the particular approach being used to study the Bible was quite good. Was she ever in for a surprise! What stood out to my wife was that the teacher never once offered an interpretation of the text under consideration. Instead, she went around the circle of people, asking each one to offer their own private interpretation of the passage. When Bonnie asked the teacher why she was not teaching the text, she responded, "To do so would be to infer that other people's interpretations are wrong. And we don't want to appear narrow-minded." So whatever sounded right to each person went unquestioned.

---

1. It is not my purpose here to unravel the maze of questions regarding what happens to an infant who dies in infancy.

The fear of being perceived as elitist and judgmental, even when teaching the clear meaning of Scripture, comes from the leaven of the philosophy of the age and its message of "tolerance."

In contrast to the Bible study my wife experienced, the apostle Peter is crystal clear when he writes, "But know this first of all, that no prophecy of Scripture is a matter of *one's own interpretation*, for no prophecy was ever made by an act of human will, but men moved by the Holy Spirit spoke from God" (2 Peter 1:20–21, italics mine). That the Bible is not a human invention but is spoken "from God," seems to be lost on a vast number of people whose interpretation of the Scriptures is limited to whatever happens to sound right.

Nobody Likes a Know-it-all

Some years ago, I attended a meeting of evangelical leaders as an advisor. The focus of the meeting was a ministry and the strategy to implement the ministry on a worldwide scale. The names of the men sitting around the giant table remain extremely well-known in evangelical circles. The more I listened in on the conversation, however, the more I became aware of the fact that no one was looking to the Bible for direction. Then I began to notice men saying things of a spiritual nature that had a ring of truth, but which struck me as non-biblical and therefore unwise.

Since I had been asked to attend the meeting in order to offer the leader of the group some insight, I decided to chime in. I raised my hand and was recognized. All eyes turned toward me. I must admit I felt rather awkward, especially in the company of such an august body of evangelical leaders. I spoke for less than a minute, expounding on what the Scriptures said in light of the topic under discussion. Now granted, there are areas of the Bible that are debatable among men of good will. But the particular point I made should have been, or so I thought, self-evident. As soon as I finished, you could have heard a pin drop. "Uh oh," I thought to myself. "I don't think these men wanted to hear that." The leader quietly thanked me for my insights while the meeting went on as if I were the invisible man.

At the close of the meeting, one of the men who had given me a funny look approached me and said something that absolutely floored me. He said, "John, nobody likes a self-assertive, know-it-all." With that, he just walked away. This is where we are today. The person who dares to question sound-right theology is a "self-assertive know-it-all." We used to be called, "Bereans" (Acts 17:11). What was the source of the cultural leaven in this particular case? Pragmatism. If a ministry stratagem promises to work, a leader will look for a proof text to support it. But if a proof text can't be found, then the Bible is expendable.

Many more examples of sound-right theology and its effect on the church's worship and witness could be provided here. But the more important question at this point is "Why are Christians so quick to believe whatever sounds right?"

BIBLICAL AGNOSTICISM

The fundamental cause of sound-right theology is that people who practice it have no thirst for absolute truth. They are practicing self-imposed ignorance about the Bible. By trading historically-verifiable, biblical thinking for subjectivist and visionary thinking we are, whether we see it or not, whether we intend it or not, drafting a new constitution for our churches, one away from the authority of the Bible toward the whims of public and spiritual consciousness. As we mix Jesus with the new paradigms of culture, before long, the new view of reality seems more normal to us than the true reality of God's Word. Again, we are wise to heed the warning of Jesus and to recall why He gave it. It's so easy to allow in the leaven of the world and not even know it.

There is a transformation of values happening in our churches and only the wise and prudent will see it for what it is. There are compromising pastors and their sheep who desire leaven for the same reason that the yeast is used—to expand dough or batter. So they are quick to inject a new form and structure for the Christian faith into church life because it too promises expansion. Some leaders shamelessly describe the manipulation behind their change as a wholly restructured view of the Church and of revelation. This is the Emergent Church movement and its offspring. While the average churchman is perhaps not interested in reinventing church, he is, nonetheless, spiritually complacent and compliant enough to "go with the flow" when he feels the cultural peer pressure to choose between being effective (as the world defined "effective) and being biblical. But beware. There is a cost attached to the leaven of unbiblical, subjectivist thinking—a destructive influence that in time totally corrupts its host.

True effectiveness in ministry comes through Jesus Christ and His powerful working through His Word and Spirit. But that's not what the majority of people today seem eager to hear. Seeking suitable truths that validate their visions, they spurn the foundational things of God. Long ago, God described this folly. "Woe to the rebellious children," declares the LORD, "Who execute a plan, but not Mine, and make an alliance, but not of My Spirit, in order to add sin to sin" (Isaiah 30:1).

But then He provides the answer, the way out of the morass of compromised religion. "For thus the Lord GOD, the Holy One of Israel, has said, 'In repentance and rest you will be saved, in quietness and trust is your strength'" (v. 15). To this He adds, "Therefore the LORD longs to be gracious to you, and therefore He waits on high to have compassion on you for the LORD is a God of justice; how blessed are all those who long for Him" (v. 18).

THE PROPER MIX OF CHRISTIAN AND SECULAR

Before we end this chapter, let me offer what I hope will be some helpful examples, again from church history, regarding the right way to go about utilizing secular ideas, themes, and symbols for Christian usage. It's through *reforming* them.

Early Christian Art

The idea habitually put forth is that once Christianity received its grant of temporal liberty as a consequence of Constantine's religious reforms, the Church quickly grew to feel "at home" in the world whereby it became complacent and spiritually soft. This point has merit. Nonetheless, there is evidence to imply that this view cannot be taken as a generalization of the church of the fourth century.

To prove this point let's examine some examples of early Christian art. The art of Christian antiquity accommodated many symbols from Roman popular culture. But Christians utilized these themes in a positive way. The figure of Jonah in a state of repose from the famed "Jonah sarcophagus" uses a standardized pagan form that was likely used in both Christian and non-Christian art creations. Christians borrowed this secular form, but were careful to interpret it according to its original, biblical meaning. The result was a Christian cultural model that expressed the hope of salvation found in Christ alone.

Christian catacomb art, created after 313, demonstrates a capacity for the use of symbols associated with Roman popular piety. One of the well-preserved series of wall paintings is found in a fourth-century catacomb on the Via Latina, discovered as recently as 1956. It's believed to have been a private burial site for a small number of families. Via Latina serves as an excellent example of how Christian art, after the ascension of Constantine, embarked on a proper synthesis of pagan and Christian cultural ideas.

For example, in room N of the burial chamber we see *Hercules in the Garden of the Hesperides*, a theme taken from pagan mythology. But in room L we find *Samson and the Lion*. How do we explain this juxtaposition of pagan and Christian motifs? Did Christians of the period embrace the universalistic claims and pretensions of the Roman gods that they could provide salvation? Or was their selective use of pagan themes intended to create competition with the time-honored religions of the Empire? According to the former opinion (which is the traditional view), the earliest Christian art was closely akin to the arts of the Oriental cults because, so it's said, Christianity itself was in large part a conventional mystery religion.[2]

However, the scriptural nature of Christian theology and the Christian use of the Bible as a sourcebook for the creation and interpretation of art images suggest the latter view. *A technique of Christian art of the period was to contrast a Christian theme with a pagan one in order to demonstrate the superiority of the one over the other.* A similar technique was to use a symbol from Roman popular piety as an element in a Christian composition in order to articulate the same message. Therefore, the assorted religious depictions in the burial chamber at Via Latina, most likely painted by the same artist, are a conspicuous attempt to say that Samson is the Christian Hercules, who is *superior* to the pagan god.

The same emphasis comes to light as we move into Cubiculum O at Via Latina where we find the *Raising of Lazarus*. The composition presents Christ as a large, senatorial, Apollo-type figure. In Roman times Apollo stood for power. But why model Christ after a pagan god? Again, we can conjecture that Christians were simply comfortable with the use of pagan similes in their art, or we can detect in its use a hidden meaning: in this case a declaration of Christ's superiority over the Roman Apollo as a deliverer from death.

2. See Jas Elsner, *Imperial Rome and Christian Triumph: The Art of the Roman Empire A.D. 100–450* (Oxford: Oxford University Press, 1998).

The latter interpretation is supported by the fact that in the ancient world the idea of the resurrection of the body was not generally accepted. For example, the Stoics and the Epicureans both denied the resurrection from the dead. What sense would it have made to paint Christ in a burial chamber in the form of a god that couldn't raise people from the dead? The borrowing of the pagan motif is intended to create pure confrontation with the Roman god. Its use is intended to say that Christ is better than Apollo. He can do what Apollo can't do—raise people from the dead.[3]

Martin Luther and Secular Tunes

For yet another example of how to reform secular themes for Christian use, let's fast forward to the sixteenth century. A great deal of controversy has been generated over Luther's adaptation of secular music, especially his use of a "bar tune" for the basis for the famous hymn, "A Mighty Fortress is Our God." Some writers insist that none of the works dealing with Luther's music can trace a single melody of his back to a drinking song and that, in fact, Luther was particularly careful in protecting the Word of God from any mixture of worldly elements. They go on to say that we have confused Luther's use of bar tunes with the fact that he wrote hymns using the metrical bar AAB or "bar-form" structure. Bar tune; bar structure. You see the problem.

However, I've found that people's adverse reaction to the marriage of secular tunes with spiritual words comes from their personal dislike for such a practice rather than from historical research. The fact is, "A particularly important class of chorales were the *contrafacta*, or parodies of secular songs, in which the given melody was retained but the text was either replaced by completely new words or else was altered so as to give it a properly spiritual meaning. The adaptation of secular songs and secular polyphonic compositions for church purposes was common in the sixteenth century."[4]

Examples of beautiful *contrafacta* include O Welt, ich muss dich lassen (O world, I now must leave thee), taken from Isaac's Lied, *Innsbruck, I now must leave thee*. A tune from Hassler's Lied *Mein Gmuth ist mir*

---

3. Portions of this section draw from my book, *The Road From Eden* (Academica Press, 2008), 33–34.

4. Donald J. Grout, *A History of Western Music*, revised edition (New York: W. W. Norton and Company, 1973), 255.

verwirret (My piece of mind is shattered by a tender maiden's charms), was changed around 1600 to *Herzlich thut mich verlangen* (My heart is filled with longing) and later to *O Haupt voll Blut und Wunden* (O sacred head now wounded).[5]

So there's no doubt that Luther exploited secular tunes for Christian worship and did so in a right way. This is in stark contrast to how so many of our churches have permitted the icons of the present culture to exploit them.

As we move into the final chapters of this book, I want to continue to concentrate on solutions to our problems. What does the future hold for Protestant evangelicalism in the West? The fact is that God is not done with us.

5. Ibid.

9

The Way Back

"One of the things we desperately need is a spiritual renewal in this country. We need a spiritual revival in America."

—BILLY GRAHAM

SPIRITUAL AWAKENING IS ON the horizon. Though the beginning of this book stated that modern evangelicalism is dying, God is coming again in Holy Ghost power to revive His people. God is already at work raising a people with a Christ-centered, Christ-grounded, and Christ-focused theology and manner of life. This move of God will bring reformation to many churches, ignite personal and proclamation evangelism, convert scores of people—many of whom have been members of churches for years—and kick off a fresh wave of missionary activity. The concerned Protestant is therefore incorrect to interpret the swelling tide of worldliness, which is now overtaking our churches, as the final word. No power on earth can resist almighty God when He flexes His awakening muscle.

This very moment God is preparing a generation of people like John the Baptist, reared in the wilderness, who truly grasp the anointing of the Holy Spirit and are fathered, mentored, and taught by God Himself through servants who proclaim His Truth. Their theology will be both scriptural and supernatural. They will feed on the works of the Reformers of old while contending for the wonders of Acts, not for the sake of spectacle, but for the unveiling of a Living, Holy God who can only be beheld through the sin-demolishing blood of Jesus Christ, the Son and Savior. It all goes back to the cross, however. When that becomes central in the body of Christ again, the sleeping giant, the Church, will arise and will be one army, united behind one cause—the glory of God in the face of Jesus Christ.

How will God bring revival? God will bring it precisely the way He's done it in the past. He will cleanse the house of Israel of its cultural carnality and vindicate His name among the nations. He will commission and send Spirit-filled preachers, evangelists of His Word, who will call His people to true repentance, faith, and holiness of life. Feeling the point of God's Sword, cutting "as far as the division of soul and spirit, of both joints and marrow, and able to judge the thoughts and intentions of the heart" (Hebrews 4:12), multitudes of lost people, many of whom have warmed the pews for years, will feel a deep anxiety over the lost and wayward condition of their souls. They'll be shaken to the core of their being over their spiritual complacency for the lost. They'll cling only to Christ as the anchor of their souls. They'll return to the Bible as the Word of God, inerrant, inspired, and authoritative.

We will not be a people who pray, but a people *of prayer*. Not a people who worship, but a people *of worship*. Not be a people who read the Book, but a people *of the Book*. In this special season, we will embrace the "words in red"—which we've conveniently quarantined under the "hard sayings of Jesus"—the way an asthmatic embraces oxygen. The waste places shall be restored. The ancient fields replanted. He will put a "new Spirit" within us. No longer will we permit the culture to set the agenda for the Church. The Church will again set the agenda for the culture. And repentance will be deep. Not a mere "change of mind." Men and women will loathe themselves in His sight for their iniquities and their abominations (for this emphasis see Ezekiel 36:22–38).

God Has Done It Before

If you doubt my anticipation of a great coming revival, then consider the following historical facts. The sixteenth-century European Reformation had a profound impact on virtually every area of European life. It literally transformed Europe. However, the spiritual danger facing Europe of the early seventeenth century was one that the magisterial Reformers Luther and Calvin would not have predicted. The rising sun of the Reformation that had shown such promise of being the standard-bearer of the light of the gospel to the nations had, within just several decades of their deaths, been eclipsed by a false gospel—the "light" of reason. In the hands of Descartes and Locke, this light was said to aid men in their search for the truth of Christianity. In the hands of Tillotson and Toland, however, this light became the grid through which all revelation was to be judged. In some cases the light of reason was little more than a warmed-over paganism reminiscent of the state-mandated religion of Rome.

By the mid-eighteenth century, the gloves were off. When Voltaire and Rousseau referred to their activities as promoting the "Enlightenment," they meant that they were replacing what they perceived as the darkness, ignorance, and grip of Christianity that had ruled men's minds from the Middle Ages to the Thirty Years War with the "light" of human reason, autonomy, and tolerance.

It took but a short time for the doctrines of the Enlightenment to reach the shores of America. By the late-eighteenth century, the "best and brightest" of our still young nation were being captivated by its seductive grip. It's believed that by the time Timothy Dwight became the 8th President of Yale in 1795, there were fewer than twenty Christians in the entire college. Yet did God wring His hands in desperation? No. In response to the prayers, fasting, and supplications of godly men and women in Scotland and America, He raised up mighty, Spirit-filled preachers of the gospel, men such as Daniel Baker and Asahel Nettleton, to usher in the Second Great Awakening.

GOD: THE CHANGE-AGENT

Of course, my prediction of a coming revival begs the question, "What causes revival?" Many churches have an annual "Spring revival." After it's over, however, most of the people are just as spiritually parched as they were before the revival started. The fact is that you can't plan a revival. I recall many years ago, going to preach protracted meetings in Virginia, not far from Charlottesville. As I was driving to the church, I passed another church. To my utter amazement, the church's marquee read, "Miracles at 8:00 p.m." *Miracles at 8:00 p.m.?* I thought. What if God wants to do a miracle at 7:45? Did anyone tell God He couldn't do miracles until 8:00?

The sign in front of that little church on the back roads of the Virginia countryside is emblematic of modern revivalism that has jettisoned the sovereignty of God in revival and has replaced it with planned, method-driven sideshow attractions no different in theory than the innovation-laden and entertainment-oriented worship services found throughout the urban sprawl of America's larger cities.

Though we should seek God for a fresh season of revival and reformation, only God—in His sovereign power and timing, wisdom, purpose, and grace—can, and will, send it. This is how revival happens. Revival can't be deliberated or whooped up. The process doesn't begin with boisterous prayers to a napping God who needs to be aroused from his slumber. God is at work before we are at work. We must pray for revival. Nonetheless, the very prayers, fastings, and supplications that stir our hearts for more of God begin with the sovereign activity of the Spirit in our hearts. *We want revival only because God wants revival.* From our human vantage point, it may appear as though we strike the match that kindles the fires of heaven-sent revival. However, it is God who inspires us to reach for the match.

Why did the Holy Spirit pour forth in power in the Congregational church in Northampton, Massachusetts in 1734 to spawn America's First Great Awakening? Why did God use Howell Harris and Daniel Rowlands to lead the Welsh Methodist revival in the eighteenth century? Why did God use William Burns and Robert Murray M'Cheyne to so severely wound the conscience of parishioners at St. Peter's Presbyterian Church in Dundee, Scotland that deep concern about sin, impending judgment, and reconciliation with God resulted in a remarkable harvest of souls in the mid-nineteenth century?

Because God decided it. There is no other explanation.

Certainly one might argue that God sends seasons of revival because His people need it. If the Old Testament teaches us anything, it's that no sooner does God do miracles in our lives, and inspire us to a renewed faith, than we're back to faithlessly complaining about our want, demonstrating our need for Him to dispose unto us again His awakening Spirit. Yet, is it not true that this back-and-forth pattern from faith to disbelief is always present among God's people? In the final analysis, God's sovereignty alone explains the where and the when of awakening grace.

THE CRY TO GOD

But let's not forget the equal truth of human responsibility. Though historical revival is at God's discretion, His prerogative is not to the exclusion of His people seeking Him for it, as I've said. God is still on His throne and delights to bare His mighty arm in revival when His people get *serious* with Him. Conscientiously and prayerfully knocking on the door of heaven for revival, and preaching its principles from the pulpit, is emphasized in Scripture. The Psalmist pleads, "O God, restore us and cause Your face to shine upon us, and we will be saved" (Psalm 80:3). Again, the Psalmist implores, "Restore us, O God of our salvation, and cause Your indignation toward us to cease. Will You be angry with us forever? Will You prolong Your anger to all generations? Will You not Yourself revive us again, that Your people may rejoice in You? Show us Your lovingkindness, O LORD, and grant us Your salvation" (Psalm 85:4–7).

The heart-felt cry of the Psalmist is today being echoed in little prayer gatherings all across the land. May we all, with earnest resignation before God, cry out to Him for a fresh, heaven-sent blessing of His Spirit.

A Grave Concern

But how serious are we? Could it be that God will not send revival upon us until and unless we are dead set on pursuing Him for it? And could it be that we won't see the importance of our need for revival until we are stripped of everything? My wife, Bonnie, once commented to me, "We just need a good persecution in this country." She meant that as long as all is well with us we tend not to go hard after God. But as soon as life takes a turn for the worse, our knees hit the floor. Maybe, for once, God just needs to keep us down long enough so that we'll get the message. Maybe then we'll turn toward heaven, this time remaining on our faces until God sends a unique season of refreshment. Are we willing to say to God, "Do whatever it takes in my life, in our nation; bring whatever natural disaster you deem necessary to strip away the curse of modernity so that we can experience revival?" Are we willing to pay the price for revival?

DEFINING "REVIVAL"

How will we know when revival comes? When you go to pick someone up at the airport, it always helps to know what the person looks like so you're not standing around the luggage area holding up a card with their name scrolled across it. What does revival look like so that when it arrives we'll recognize it? Does it have a specific profile that makes it easily identifiable?

The word "revival" is a particularly vague word in evangelical church life. It conjures up images of the annual revival, in which a visiting evangelist is invited to speak. Or it can refer to specific historical happenings, such as the Welsh revival of 1904–1905 in which the Methodist preacher, Joseph Jenkins, encouraged all "to deepen our loyalty to Christ." Discovering a strict definition of revival from the Bible, and one that is discernible in history, is crucial if we are to pray and seek God wisely for it.

Important Distinction

But before I offer a definition of revival, let's first differentiate "awakening" and "revival." They're not one and the same. While it's common to say that a spiritual awakening occurs among non-Christians, producing mass conversions, and that revival happens among Christians who have turned apathetic, it's best to say that *spiritual awakening is a sovereign movement of God's Spirit that produces revival among both unbelievers and believers.* In other words, awakening and revival are flip sides of the same coin. They can't be surgically separated. When the awakening power of the Holy Spirit moves, non-Christians become Christians, and Christians who have grown indifferent to God, and to His mission, repent.

Now let's look for a clear biblical definition of revival.

The Biblical Record

Exodus 3 and 4:17 record God's call to Moses to deliver the children of Israel out of the land of Egypt. The call of God is the basis for Moses' legitimacy as a leader of God's people. Moses, and no one else, led the Israelites out of Egypt, delivered the 10 Commandments to the people, and called them to repentance because his legitimacy as a leader gave him the authority to do these things.

After decades of wandering in the wilderness, the nation of Israel is now about to enter the Promised Land. Chapters 29 and 30 of the book of Deuteronomy comprise the last portion of Moses' third and final discourse to the Jewish people prior to his death in Jordan and their entering the Promised Land under the leadership of Joshua. It's here that Moses, as God's legitimate leader, reviews the Law first given at Sinai, calling the people to turn from idols and to keep the Law, which is magnificently summed up in the words of Moses, "I call heaven and earth to witness against you today, that I have set before you life and death, the blessing and the curse. So choose life in order that you may live, you and your descendants" (Deuteronomy 30:19).

In Joshua 24, Joshua and the people are gathered together at Shechem, the place where God made a covenant with Abraham and promised to give the land to his descendants (Genesis 12:1–9). Joshua, having been called by God to lead the people, recalls the promises made to Abraham, and he cleanses Jacob's house once more. Joshua can do this because his legitimacy as a leader gave him the authority to call the people to repentance.

When Josiah ascended the throne, he instituted a series of reforms, which included reformation of the city and the nation, the reinstitution of the Passover celebration in the Temple, and the refurbishing of the Temple itself. 2 Chronicles 34 records that during the time the Temple was being restored to a place of honor, Hilkiah the priest found the Book of the Law delivered by Moses. When the faithful King Josiah read the Book of the Covenant before the people of Judah, a great revival took place. "Josiah removed all the abominations from all the lands belonging to the sons of Israel, and made all who were present in Israel to serve the Lord their God. Throughout his lifetime they did not turn from following the Lord God of their fathers" (2 Chronicles 34:33). Josiah was able to do these things because his legitimacy as a leader gave him the authority to call the people to repentance.

Having heard the devastating report that the walls of Jerusalem were torn down, her gates burned with fire, and the survivors left in deep distress, Nehemiah, the cupbearer of the King, turned his face toward God and prayed according to the covenant, confessing his sin and that of his father's house. In answer to Nehemiah's prayer, King Artaxerxes permitted him to return to Judah to begin the activity of rebuilding. When Nehemiah returned to help the Jews rebuild the gates in the Jerusalem wall, he led the people in revival by assembling the people and having the Law read for three full hours a day (Nehemiah 8–10). Nehemiah was able to do this because his legitimacy as a leader gave him the authority to call the people to repentance.

In each of the cases cited above, and we could review many more throughout the pages of the Bible, we see that revival is the result of *renewing the covenant.* Taking into consideration the other points I've made, I'll define revival more fully this way. *Revival is the result of God's*

legitimate leaders calling people back to the Word of God, whereby people
repent and follow God with their whole hearts, souls, minds, and strength.
When this happens, we'll know that revival has come.

God's Servants in Revival

Who does God generally use to bring revival? God may use a notable
ruler like Josiah to spearhead revival, but more often than not, the Bible
shows that God uses the least likely people. He could very well use you!
God gave His covenant Law, which said in part, "Do not murder." Who
did God entrust to deliver His law? Moses, a murderer. Nehemiah was
the cupbearer to the King. Samson was a serial adulterer. Hosea was
married to an unfaithful woman, and Amos was a mere shepherd and
a grower of figs. Jonah's only claim to fame was that he was the son of
Ammitai. And all the disciples of Jesus were but common men. Why
then are so many men in the ministry "positioning themselves" to be
the next great pastor? Often God revives His people using the refuse, the
menial workers, the weak, the wounded, and the outcast. He does this so
that the glory will go to Him, not to man.

WHY GOD SENDS REVIVAL

I've been poked fun at for my belief in a great coming revival. "You must
be kidding," one friend said to me. "You don't understand the extent to
which the spirit of anti-Christ has taken over the West. Europe is finished, and America is not far behind." Well, I stand by my belief. I take
as the basis of my position a single verse buried in the pages of Ezekiel's
prophesy. The prophet declares, "Therefore say to the house of Israel,
'Thus says the Lord GOD, "It is not for your sake, O house of Israel,
that I am about to act, but for My holy name, which you have profaned
among the nations where you went"'" (Ezekiel 36:22). How ought we to
understand these words?

    In the previous chapter, we learned that by attempting to couple
the man-centered trends of culture with the blessings of God's covenant
promises, ancient Israel sinned grievously against God and suffered
many years for it in Babylonian captivity. But while in foreign captivity
something happened. The people of Israel became a source of ridicule.
The pagan nations, who knew of Israel's glorious past as the conqueror
of Canaan and that Israel's God was the Lord, began to mock and jeer.

God's people became a "byword" (Daniel 9:16), an object of scorn among the nations.

Far worse, because Israel was God's covenant people, by association God's name was derided. As the laughing and jeering of the name of God rose higher and higher to heaven, God was moved to action. He never lets His name be profaned for long. He released His people from captivity and reinstated them to their homeland. In the same chapter of Ezekiel, God promises to vindicate His greatness by restoring Israel and making them clean (v. 25), giving them a new heart (v. 26), and putting His Spirit in them to cause them to be obedient (v. 27). So, God saved His people, not for their sakes, but *for His name's sake*. He restored His people to restore the integrity of His name among the nations.

We can therefore expect another great revival not because God feels that people are deserving of His grace, but because He is jealous over His name. God is always primed and ready to send a season of refreshing upon His people in order to prove Himself holy among the nations of world.

To Bless God

Now for those who are conscious of the great need for revival and reformation, and pray accordingly, there's a side point I'd like to share. When we pray for spiritual awakening, are not our minds tuned to the blessings that such a move of the Spirit will bring to *us* rather than to God? Do we ever think about how the people's sluggishness to pray, evangelize, and to seek the God of heaven with all heart, mind, soul, and strength drags the mighty name of God through the mud? Are we discerning enough to realize that the reason we ought to seek God for revival is so that we should not profane the name of the Lord any longer? That we might again become a means by which God can lionize His holy name? Without the glory of God as our goal for revival and reformation, our desire for it remains man-centered.

THE NECESSITY FOR REVIVAL

Why do we need revival? We need churches full of people who have experienced true, Holy Spirit inspired conversion and who are thus people sold out for Christ. Lots of churches have touched communities, but not by the power of God. It's a fact that what a lot of churches call "accomplishment" in ministry really goes to the credit of human activity, colorful personalities behind the pulpit, church-growth techniques, and professionalism, not the wind of the Spirit. Consequently, we've convinced many of the beauty of our church, but not of its Head. Lack of true conversions is the unfortunate result.

Duncan Campbell noticed the urgent need for Holy Ghost inspired revival in his own day when he so insightfully remarked, "Today, we have a Christianity made easy as an accommodation to an age that is unwilling to face the implication of Calvary, and the gospel of 'simple believism' has produced a harvest of professions which have done untold harm to the cause of Christ."[1]

I also think of those pastors and church leaders, many gifted men, whom I've known over the years who've remained faithful to God's ways in the ministry but who have seen so little fruit. They preach the joy of the Lord but walk in quiet desperation. They look back over years of preaching, teaching, and much labor on a variety of levels, and what do they see? No memorial stones of victory commemorating neighborhoods changed by the gospel, no church life pulsating with zeal for God's house. The land remains scorched and the thirsty ground yet yearns for springs of water.

Yes, we need God's awakening hand to send a fresh season of revival. And we need to see it followed by reformation so that the fruit of revival will last. These things don't come by the means of human skill or competence. They aren't a product that can be manufactured on the assembly line of human ingenuity and novelty. They come because God says so. But they also come when men and women find that place of humility before a Holy God and cry out as the Baptist, "He must increase, but I must decrease" (John 3:30).

Until, like Nehemiah, we grieve over the lost condition of mankind; until, like Paul, we see our own guilt of doing what we shouldn't do, and not doing the things we ought to do; until, like Jonathan Edwards, we're broken over the worldliness and weakness of our churches as a whole; we may, like King Saul, continue to look good on the outside but shall continue to decay spiritually on the inside.

1. Duncan Campbell, *1949 Revival in the Hebrides Islands, Scotland,* http://www .firesofrevival.com/trevival/dcrchap07.htm The book is currently out of print, but for now can be found online at http://firesofrevival.com/trevival/dcrevival.htm

In a time of extreme spiritual apathy among Christian people, let's come before God with true conviction, a deepening hunger for a heaven-sent revival. Let's be anxious about the attitude of the Church in general, which has replaced aggressive evangelism with whatever effort it takes to get people through the door, or with no evangelism at all because there is so little heartfelt care for the lost. Indeed, let us draw near to the throne of grace with souls heavily burdened and longing for a fresh manifestation of God such that the words of our mouths echo those of the prophet Isaiah,

> Oh, that You would rend the heavens and come down,
> That the mountains might quake at Your presence—
> As fire kindles the brushwood, as fire causes water to boil—
> To make Your name known to Your adversaries,
> That the nations may tremble at Your presence!
> When You did awesome things which we did not expect,
> You came down, the mountains quaked at Your presence.
> For from days of old they have not heard or perceived by ear,
> Nor has the eye seen a God besides You,
> Who acts in behalf of the one who waits for Him (Isaiah 64:1–4).

Given what we've learned to this point, it should take little to see that for a spiritual awakening to ignite our churches and transform our contiguous culture, indeed, for evangelicalism to be a God-glorifying movement once more, there is one thing, above all else, that we must recover: the gospel. No revival or reformation has ever occurred in history without the gospel message taking a central role. Although the reader may have more interest in some sort of plan or program for revitalizing the churches, I shall offer only the thought that to recapture and live out fully the gospel is to automatically set a host of things right. So, what are the fundamental truths of the gospel? We'll explore this question in the next chapter.

10

Raising the Dead

"Blush, my soul, that you have exchanged the divine for a bestial likeness; blush that despite your heavenly origin you now wallow in filth."

—BERNARD OF CLAIRVAUX

THE GOSPEL MESSAGE BEGINS with the fact that all people are born totally dead in sin. The apostle is clear as crystal when he declares, "You were dead in your trespasses and sins" (Ephesians 2:1). What does Paul mean by "dead?" Dead means dead. How dead? Completely dead. The non-Christian isn't like a drowning man. He's like a man lying at the bottom of the ocean with his eyes X'd out. He's not in need of assistance, but resurrection.

The Need for This Doctrine

Why is an embrace of this truth so important in order for our churches to experience true and lasting revival? *We cannot grasp the fullness of salvation in Christ until we first grasp the fullness of death in us.* There are various weaknesses in the evangelical movement, but none are as feeble as the thought that the Kingdom of God can be established and spread by new *techniques* designed to reach people. By elevating style over substance or, better yet, the method of ministry over the message of ministry, church leaders have effectively inoculated people from God's revelation of the unmitigated corruption of their hearts. Sadly, in many of the churches, Jesus is an afterthought. He's the life-enhancer instead of the sinner-Redeemer.

Unless the Word of God exposes people's sin, they will not see the total supremacy of Christ for salvation and sanctification. Without seeing this, our churches are fated to remain man-centered institutions of religiosity, devoid of the power of the Holy Spirit. As long as people are shielded from the truth of the total depravity of their hearts, their lives will continue to experience no real and lasting change and our churches will persist in having no real and lasting impact upon our culture.

Do you believe that people are born dead in sin? If not, why then do you think we live in a dying culture? Why is there no fear of God before this generation? It's because we haven't warned our children that because of their sinful hearts the wrath of God is upon them. New mothers, do you believe that the fetus you carry is hell-bound unless the Spirit of God causes it to be born again? Do you hold fast to the truth that only the Holy Spirit can change your child's future?

IMPORTANT DEFINITIONS AND CLARIFICATIONS

To be clear, people are dead in sins on the basis of two realities.

First, as already noted, we are all born in sin. This is the sin nature. Paul writes of Christians that we were once "by nature children of wrath" (Ephesians 2:3). And King David records a truth which applies to all people. "Behold, I was brought forth in iniquity, and in sin my mother conceived me" (Psalm 51:5). We don't become sinners because we sin. We sin because of original sin.

Second, we all commit sin. We sin in acts, thoughts, and deeds. When we sin we "fall short of the glory of God" (Romans 3:23). Because the glory of God is the sum total of all God's perfections, to fall short of the glory of God is to fall short of God. While sin can also be defined as falling short of the Law, as embodied in the 10 Commandments, the Law is an expression of God's holy nature. Historic Christian theology distinguishes *sins of commission* (things we do, but should not have done) from *sins of omission* (things we ought to have done, but did not). But the end result is the same: sin is coming short of the perfect nature of God.

The Heart Is a Latrine

No one should depreciate the vileness of sin. Psalm 58 compares the heart of man to a "cobra" which strikes with deadly venom. Paul equates all that his heart once held dear to "dung" (Philippians 3:8). James tells us that the mouth is full of molten lava, making the tongue into a "fire" (James 3:6f). This is evidenced by the fact that we talk about brothers and sisters behind their backs while in corporate worship we bless and praise the name of God. And Jesus speaks of the heart in terms of a cesspool, from which flows "evil thoughts, fornications, thefts, murders, adulteries, deeds of coveting and wickedness, as well as deceit, sensuality, envy, slander, pride and foolishness. All these evil things proceed from within and defile the man" (Mark 7:21–23).

On the other hand, God is Holy, pure, and undefiled. Do you think that God will permit a cesspool into His undefiled heaven? Some of you are so concerned with your white couch that you cover it with plastic twelve months a year and refuse to let anyone sit on it. How much less will God allow sin into His holy heaven!

A Fateful Day

Human sin is also universal. April 16th, 2007, was a day of tragedy at Virginia Tech University. Cho Seung Hui set out from his dorm on his way to kill 32 people, and then himself, in the bloodiest mass murder by a lone gunman in American history. I recall driving home as I heard the news on my car radio. Not long after this tragedy, accusations began to fly that someone should have seen Cho's potential for havoc. His clothing, behavior, past psychological history, and especially the fact that some members of Cho's family in South Korea had expressed concern about him—all should have clued people in that this young man was a ticking time bomb just waiting to explode.

But in a real sense, Cho's attitude about life, especially his appearance and the cultural trends he bought into, are not particularly unusual. One can turn on cable TV or go on the Internet any day of the week and find the same kind of lyrics supporting anarchy and "down with society" that played a central role in shaping Cho's worldview. As alluded to earlier, much of today's youth culture celebrates images of death, the macabre, extreme introspection, and the outright rejection of social norms. It all points to the fact that sin is universal. The Bible is so true when it reminds us, "For all have sinned and fall short of the glory of God" (Romans 3:23).

God Hates Sin

Though God is patient with sinners, there comes a point when He runs out of patience. It's at this point that God gives some unrepentant sinners over to their desires, such that their behavior gets a lot worse (Romans

1:26–32). God does this because He hates sin. He loathes spiritual suicide and our enabling others in the process. Believers are to hate sin, but God's hatred of sin is a perfect hatred. Our hatred of sin is tainted by the presence of the remaining stain of sin in our lives. Our disgust over sin is therefore only ever an imperfect reflection of God's perfect disgust over sin.

Another reason God hates sin is because our sins are first and foremost against Him (Psalm 51:4). We are so easy to predict. If something doesn't affect us directly, we're prone to react less harshly. However, if it were your child killed at Virginia Tech, even as shocked as you are over what happened, you'd be a basket case. The closer tragedies hit home, the more we react with sadness, revulsion, and anger. Since all sin is principally against God, and God is perfect, His reaction to sin is at all times perfect revulsion and anger.

Judgment Day

There is an eternal penalty for sin. Christ Himself will condemn impenitent reprobates at the Judgment Seat of God and assign them to eternal flames. No personal penance or private set of morals can change this fact. The Bible contains over 580 references to God's wrath and anger, and it uses 20 different Hebrew words to describe God's anger and wrath. Because God hates sin, He plans to judge all unremorseful sinners to hell. Jesus spoke of hell as an unquenchable fire (Mark 9:43).

Of course, many people are repulsed at the idea of hell. "What do you mean I'm under God's wrath? What an archaic notion! All this talk of hell makes a loving God out to be tyrannical." Niccolo Machiavelli went as far as to mock the reality of hell. "I desire to go to hell," he quipped, "and not to Heaven. In the former I shall enjoy the company of popes, kings and princes, while in the latter are only beggars, monks and apostles." I wonder if Machiavelli is scoffing now.

WHAT IT MEANS FOR US

Consider the above facts against the backdrop of the shallowness of Christianity in the West. America is quickly following in the footsteps of Europe. What has become of the grief, the crying out to God over our sins, both personal and corporate, and also over the escalating loss of our Christian culture that is awash in sin? It's been marginalized by a new set of concerns, those which revolve around self-protectionism and personal advancement. Blinding ourselves to the need to renew the covenant with God, to see true revival happen in our generation, we've grown content with what we have and with who we are.

Do we recruit others to sin? If not, do we expose it? In our increasingly lazed approach to church discipline, we easily and conveniently see no evil, hear no evil, and fail to speak of evil in the camp. The ease with which we skirt the hard issue of sin is easily seen in how many profess the gospel but live no differently than those who profess no faith at all. The looming advance of elitist, politically-correct, non-judgmentalism is seen in our instinctive reaction to let sin slide and also in our lack of courage to believe that, with Christ in us, we can renew His Word in our own hearts and go beyond the inconsequentiality of belief to become His change-agents.

The Return of the Fireside Chat

One of the first books to be printed in the mid-fifteenth century was a short book called the *Ars Moriendi* (*Art of Dying Well*). It's been called a "do-it-yourself guide to dying well" at a time when most people died in their homes. The *Ars Moriendi* watered down the fear of death by praising death as the end of all misery and the beginning of true happiness, provided one learns how to die well. Christian readers were encouraged to die well by supervising their own spirituality over and against the top-down, command-and-control authority of the Church at Rome and by focusing on individual free will and the power to win salvation through genuine penance.

In the days when the *Ars Moriendi* was written, the Roman Catholic Church was certainly clear on the impending judgment of God after death, but the culture of the time was fighting against this teaching. In many people's minds the only thing left for people to fear was the fear of death itself. The little book did everything it could to help eliminate this fear.

Though terribly non-biblical in nature, at the very least, the *Ars Moriendi* offered its readers *some* instruction on what to do in the face of death. Problematically, a lot of our churches have held in reserve the moralistic teachings of the *Ars Moriendi* while abandoning the concern with death and, much more still, with the fear of the judgment of God after death. Today some of the world's most popular preachers, best-selling Christian books, and multitudinous small group discipleship meetings address how you can overcome the fear of aging, the fear and stress of raising kids, the fear of financial hardship, and the fear of not being a success in life, but not the fear of death and judgment. You'd think that F.D.R had returned to proclaim, "The only thing to fear is fear itself."

Don't fool yourself. God is angry with unrepentant sinners every day and has every intention to consign them to hell. But praise God, He has settled the issue of our sins irrevocably at the cross and in the glorious resurrection of Jesus from the dead (1 Corinthians 15:1–19). The depths of the human condition have been overcome by the merciful, loving, and powerful work of God through Jesus Christ. So then, the biblical way to "die well" is found in the assurance of Christ to forgive all of our sins and to give us the gift of eternal life in Him.

The question now is *how does the finished work of Christ become practical for people?* In other words, if sinners are graveyard dead and can do nothing to be saved, how can their predicament change? The answer lies in God's marvelous grace.

THE LORD OF SALVATION

Salvation is accomplished by Christ and applied to us by God's Spirit. The work of the Holy Spirit brings us into a living union with Christ. God opens our eyes, we see. God unplugs our ears, we hear. Jesus calls a dead and buried Lazarus out of the grave, he comes alive. In the same way, the Holy Spirit calls us to God, opens our spiritual eyes, and raises us to newness of life.

God declares back in the pages of the Old Testament that salvation begins with His initiating activity. "Moreover, I will give you a new heart and put a new spirit within you; and I will remove the heart of stone from your flesh and give you a heart of flesh. I will put My Spirit within you and cause you to walk in My statutes, and you will be careful to observe My ordinances" (Ezekiel 36:26–27). Jesus Himself categorically denies the possibility of a person being born again by virtue of human effort or decision when He said, "You did not choose Me but I chose you, and appointed you that you would go and bear fruit, and that your fruit would remain, so that whatever you ask of the Father in My name He may give to you (John 15:16, see also John 1:12–13, 3:1–8).

How does God start the eye-and-ear-opening process of salvation in us? Through the application of the Word of God in combination with the power of the Holy Spirit. Ezekiel's vision of the valley of dry bones remains the most vivid description of God's power to raise the spiritually dead to newness of life (Ezekiel 37:14).

Fail to understand what the Scriptures say and you're destined to repeat the errors of humanistic religion that have brought so many of our churches to the current point. Only through the supernatural working of God's Holy Spirit can one see the total depravity of one's sin before God and, thus, the all-sufficiency of Christ for salvation and for sanctification.[1]

A MISSED OPPORTUNITY

Failing to understand God's supremacy in redemption is precisely the problem in legions of Protestant churches. Rather than depend on the powerful Word of God and the sovereign Spirit to bring people to the knowledge of salvation, they continue to trust in the horses of ecclesiastical professionalism, methodological manipulation, and networking. Correspondingly, a large number of people attending these churches go untouched by the life-saving message of the gospel whereby the neighborhoods surrounding these churches continue to flounder in the recklessness of unbelief.

The sad truth, however, is that so many non-Christians who attend church, as well as those who live near our churches but who would never darken the door of a church, are looking for answers. Because their hearts are dead in sin, they're not looking for the God of the Bible. Nonetheless, the quiet desperation in which so many people live causes them to reflect on the state of their lives, their futures, their children' futures, and how— if at all possible—they can change their lives for the better. It's high time we return to total trust in God's saving power and become ambassadors of His great gospel to the world.

---

1. Many people don't like the idea that God's love precedes man's love in salvation. They insist that sin has made man sick but not entirely dead in sins. Their proof is to insist that it's folly to analogize the spiritually dead with the physically dead because just as physically dead people can't choose God, neither can they choose sin. But it's not folly because John 9 uses physical blindness as an analogy of spiritual blindness that accompanies our lost condition. Spiritual blindness is different from physical blindness, but that doesn't mean the analogy is false.

The New You?

The culture tries to encourage us to think in terms of a "new beginning" with catchy slogans like "50 is the new 40." But anyone who's 50 years of age and who's still out there trying to jog, surf, and workout at the gym as though they're still 40 (or 18!) knows that their knees, shoulders, and back never got the memo.

Just now, I stopped typing this chapter and googled the phrase, "New and Improved." My search yielded 166 million Internet sites. "New and improved" has long been a favorite phrase for advertisers wishing to highlight a product's saleability so you'll be inclined to buy. But have you ever purchased a product promising to be new and improved? I sure have and, to tell the truth, I rarely ever find a dime's worth of difference between it and the older version of the same product. So everybody wants to be younger, and everybody wants goods and services which are better than ever, and because deep down inside we all want that "second chance" or that enhanced *whatever*, we're roped in almost every time.

Unfortunately, too many of our churches are imitating the world by advertising themselves along the lines of being new and improved. Or they claim that you can be new and improved if you come for a visit. What is missing from these encounters is the sovereign grace of God which alone can transform people.

The deep sense of wanting to start over, to find something better, is a God-given urge. But that urge can only find its resting place in the God of heaven who alone can turn us into people who are really and truly new and improved. The Bible says of forgiven sinners, "Therefore if anyone is in Christ, he is a new creature; the old things passed away; behold, new things have come" (2 Corinthians 5:17).

What's more, neither church attendance, nor even church membership, can provide a guarantee of a God-inspired change in your life that will save your soul. Now certainly every Christian ought to attend church and be a member of that church. But evangelist Billy Sunday was so correct when he used to preach, "Joining the church doesn't anymore make one a Christian than entering a garage will change one into an automobile." Or as I often tell people in sermons, "Sitting in church doesn't make one a Christian anymore than sitting in a cookie jar makes one a cookie."

The church service may be professional and impressive, the preacher attractive and enchanting, the church as a whole serviceable and sensational. But without the potent encounter between the life-changing power of the Holy Spirit and people, sinners will remain in their sins, and Christians will remain babies.

TOO QUICK TO BELIEVE OTHERS ARE BELIEVERS

A vital reason this subject should arrest our attention is, as I've stated elsewhere, because a great many people who attend evangelical churches aren't Christians. Making matters worse, we're witnessing a rising apathy among Christians toward this fact. It's as if people just assume that those sitting near them are true believers. However, let's consider the following example from the Bible and its implications.

The apostle John conveys a startling story that took place when Jesus was in Jerusalem at the Passover. After turning the water into wine at Cana and cleaning the Temple, "during the feast, many *believed in His name*, observing His signs which He was doing" (John 2:23, italics mine).

Now if a number of people were to tell me that they believed in the name of Jesus after hearing me preach, I'd be very excited and praise God. But John goes on to say "But Jesus, on His part, was not entrusting Himself to them, for He knew all men, and because He did not need anyone to testify concerning man, for He Himself knew what was in man" (vss. 24–25). Jesus wouldn't entrust Himself to these supposed converts because He knew their hearts. Though they were professing His name, He knew they *weren't* true believers. He knew they weren't truly saved because He knew the Holy Spirit hadn't regenerated their spiritual hearts.

What Makes Faith Saving

In juxtaposition to what faith is not, John 3 immediately follows the story recounted above with the encounter between Jesus and Nicodemus. Here Jesus reveals to us the difference between presumptuous faith and regeneration which produces saving faith. Jesus tells Nicodemus he can't see the Kingdom of God because he's blind (v. 3). Further, by alluding to the wilderness experience as a context for His reference to eternal life (v.14), Jesus infers that this teacher of Israel is a rebel. So Nicodemus is a blind rebel, as it is with all unbelievers. The only answer for Nicodemus, indeed for all people, is to be "born of the Spirit" (v. 8). As Jesus answered Nicodemus, "Truly, truly, I say to you, unless one is born of water and the Spirit he cannot enter into the kingdom of God" (v.5).

So You Say You're a Christian?

Given what we just learned in John, isn't it abundantly clear that one of the great deficiencies of our churches is the quickness with which we entrust ourselves to those who say they believe? If you say you believe, but Jesus doesn't believe that you believe, then why should I believe you? Jesus warned, "Many will say to Me on that day, 'Lord, Lord, did we not prophesy in Your name, and in Your name cast out demons, and in Your name perform many miracles?' "And then I will declare to them, 'I never knew you; depart from me, you who practice lawlessness'" (Matthew 7:22–23).

I should believe you because the Spirit of regeneration has radically changed you, given you the gift of faith, has placed within you the Spirit of holiness, and you are bringing forth fruit in keeping with your repentance. What has become of this set of expectations in the churches of today?

The Word of Faith, or Prosperity Gospel, movement set the stage for the advent of the seeker-friendly, ear-tickling churches of this day and age that seems to be all about us—us being healed for comfort's sake; us being wealthy for comfort's sake; us enjoying "our best life now." In truth, our purpose is to proclaim God's message, no matter what kind of life we have on this earth. We are called to be ambassadors of another age, another realm, and to suffer for it if need be. Our "best life" only comes in intimate proximity to Almighty God. And that is only attainable through the blood of Jesus. Yet, few preachers ever even mention sin, believing there is some iota of good within man, as if he is able to just "come to his senses" and receive Christ on his own. We are losing the full dimension of the gospel—Jesus, the Savior of sinners. Otherwise, what is the gospel, and why does its truth and revelation incite us to follow this Jesus Christ with whole heart, mind, soul, and strength?

It's in view of God's mercy toward us in Christ alone that we are to offer up our lives as living sacrifices (Romans 12:1). This call is meaningless to us unless we grasp what His mercy means in regard to our hopeless, helpless estate. People are clamoring for comfort or crying out for signs and wonders. I wholeheartedly believe God wants to release His awesome power into the earth and radically revive the bride of Christ. The problem is the gospel is not being preached, sin is not being exposed, and God is not about to entrust an immature, carnal Church with Kingdom resources. Unless and until "Christ and Him crucified"—and all of it applied to us on the basis of unmerited favor—is the central message of the Church, we will remain where we are: self-focused and powerless.

Our Task

Is there hope for the dead spiritual bones of compromised evangelicalism? For nations that don't know God and are therefore in need of spiritual awakening? Indeed! Pray, preach, and teach for nothing short of a Third Great Awakening. Look for God to strip away the deadness to spiritual things, the false bravado, and smugness toward the biblical gospel found not only in our culture, but also, sadly, in too many of our churches. Pray that, by the grace of God, the "wise and intelligent" will flee to the Savior from the judgment to come. Pray for your family. Pray for your community. Be burdened for the culture that continues to flounder in the recklessness of unbelief. Without God's Spirit moving across the waters of our lives, where will our children and our grandchildren be years from now should the Lord tarry? Perhaps your prayers ought to begin with yourself.

The regenerated heart is one that turns to God in repentance and in faith, subjects to which we will now turn.

11

Pulling the Plug on Hot-Tub Christianity

"Behold, as for the proud one, His soul is not right within him;
But the righteous will live by his faith."

—Habakkuk

Biblical teaching on repentance has been all but lost in the vanguard church of today. The call of God heard throughout the pages of both the Old and New Testaments—that we are to turn from our sins to the Living God—has gradually become viewed as an impediment to our campaign to advance the image of our churches in the eyes of the world. Books that lay out how to become a better you or experience your best life now prop up modern man while begging the question of sin and the pang of guilt and shame that must be addressed if modern man is to find true healing from the disease of sin that ravages his soul. The decomposition of the modern evangelical message begins at the same point where the composition of Jesus' first public pronouncement begins. "The time is fulfilled, and the kingdom of God is at hand; repent and believe in the gospel" (Mark 1:15).

THE 180-DEGREE TURN

What is repentance? *Repentance is a work of God in our hearts whereby we turn from sin to Christ who is Lord and Savior.*[1] It's been said many times that repentance means a "change of mind." Certainly this definition is suggested by a close analysis of the Greek word *metanoeo*, which is a compound word: *meta*, meaning "a change from within," and *noeo*,

---

1. Notice I didn't write "as Lord and Savior," for Christ is not the image of a Lord and Savior. He *is* Lord and Savior.

which is derived from the Greek word *gnosis*, meaning "knowledge." In other words, change what you know, change your mind. But to change your mind, in the biblical sense of the word, is not like reaching for the crackers at the store but in mid-stream grabbing for the cookies instead. The essential nature of the word infers a vigorous and thorough willingness to amend ones behavior with absolute abhorrence over one's deceitful heart and the sins it has produced. It means a genuine, Holy-Spirit empowered resolve to stop practicing the very things for which Christ died. To repent means to change not only our thinking, but also our actions.

The Distressed Soul

Preceding repentance is deep and godly sorrow for sins. Paul writes, "For the sorrow that is according to the will of God produces a repentance without regret, leading to salvation, but the sorrow of the world produces death" (2 Corinthians 7:10). Note that godly sorrow *leads* to repentance. Sorrow and repentance are not one and the same. It's Spirit-ignited sorrow that occasions repentance.

So, sorrow is not a small thing. It's a very solemn work of the Holy Spirit. Central to godly sorrow is the experience of two things: *grief and grieving*. Recognizing the abominable nature of sin before God, the *uneasy soul* feels great grief regarding its sinful attitudes and actions. Grief then produces *grieving*. This is the outwardly *troubled heart* that shows remorse over sin, often with tears.

Whom We Have Offended

Grief and grieving are crucial aspects of repentance because the Holy Spirit *reveals* to us that our sins are first and foremost against God. Psalm 51, which I shall go to once more, stands as a biblical model for a godly sorrow that produces true repentance. "Against You, You only, I have sinned and done what is evil in Your sight, so that You are justified when You speak and blameless when You judge" (v. 4). Moreover, the depth of David's repentance is seen in his sorrow over his sin nature, which is the wellspring of all sin. "Behold, I was brought forth in iniquity and in sin my mother conceived me" (v. 5). The prayer comes to a head in David's poignant cry as he now turns to God for mercy, "Create in me a clean heart, O God, and renew a steadfast spirit within me" (v. 10).

To sum up, I'll share this wonderful definition of repentance provided us by a catechism for children produced during the time of the European Reformation. It captures everything I've said to this point. Question 87 asks, "What is repentance unto life?" The answer: "Repentance unto life is a saving grace, whereby a sinner, out of a true sense of his sin, and apprehension of the mercy of God in Christ, doth, with grief and hatred of his sin, turn from it unto God, with full purpose of, and endeavor after, new obedience."[2]

THE MARROW CONTROVERSY

The subject of repentance has been a source of disagreement dating back many years. The year was 1717. William Craig stood before the Scottish Presbytery of Auchterarder to undergo ordination trials. During the course of the proceedings, he was asked to subscribe to this statement, "It is not sound and orthodox to teach that we must forsake sin in order to our coming to Christ." He would not affirm this statement known as the Auchterarder Creed, which essentially asks, "Must a person forsake his sins in order to come to Christ?" At issue was the question of repentance. The men of the Presbytery were split over the issue. Emerging from this split, two distinct groups formed.

The Marrow Men[3] said grace always precedes faith and repentance. Thus, repentance is not a condition of the gospel offer, nor is it to be considered a condition of salvation. Repentance was not, in their minds, a cause or a condition of grace, but always a consequence of grace.

The Neonomians, on the other hand, viewed the New Testament gospel as a "new law," which replaced the Old Testament law. Essential to this law, so they held, was that faith and repentance must be met *before* God offers salvation. In other words, they placed salvation *in escrow*—maintaining that Christ doesn't save until the specific condition of abandoning sin has been met. The Marrow Men, including Thomas Boston, Ralph Erskine, and Ebenezer Erskine, replied that only by the sovereign power of Christ working mightily in us can we forsake sin. Now, the

---

2. The definition is from The Westminster Shorter Catechism.

3. Central to the debate was a book by Edward Fisher, called *The Marrow of Modern Divinity* (originally published in London as *The Marrow* in 1645, it was later reprinted in 1718 by James Hog under the new title). The short book articulated the same view of free grace that Boston and the Erskines were preaching.

Marrow Men weren't denying the need for repentance; they simply saw it as a fruit of grace.

Interesting as all this may be, the important point is that while we see great division between the Marrow Men and the Neonomians regarding the order of grace and repentance in the process of salvation, both camps were in agreement on at least one thing: the necessity for sinners to repent of their sins.

Great Awakenings Divided

Eighteenth-century Calvinists like Jonathan Edwards or George Whitefield, who were pivotal figures in America's First Great Awakening, following the Marrow men, also had stressed man's sinful nature and utter powerlessness to overcome this nature without the direct action of the grace of God working through the Holy Spirit. Nineteenth-century evangelical revivalists like Charles G. Finney, Lyman Beecher, and Francis Asbury, key people in America's Second Great Awakening, agreed with their Calvinist counterparts on the terrible sinfulness of humans, but openly proclaimed man's ability to turn away from sinful behavior and embrace Christ for salvation. Most nineteenth-century revivalists, regardless of their church affiliation, preached the duty and ability of sinners to repent and cease from sin.[4]

Again, though we see great division regarding which comes first— God's grace or repentance—like the Marrow Men and the Neonomians before them, the Calvinist and Arminian preachers agreed on at least one thing: the necessity for sinners to repent of their sins. Calvin, Arminius, Luther, Edwards, Whitefield, Wesley, Nettleton, and Finney, regardless

---

4. The centerpiece of Finney's revivalism was the conversion experience. I want to stress the word "experience." He didn't preach conversion as the result of Divine grace, but as an experience one could have if one met certain conditions, e.g. change his own heart by fully repenting of his sins and surrendering unconditionally to God's will for his life. Should a person do this, he could expect the moment of conversion to follow, in which a merciful God would bestow his grace, forgive his sins, and grant him the gift of eternal life. Finney worked hard to bring about this moment in the hearts and souls of his hearers, preaching in such a way as to produce in people a state of spiritual concern over the dire state of their souls, a frightening awareness of the prospect of hell, an unmistakable sense of conviction, and the heartfelt realization that unless some change occurred one would stand justly condemned for sins and incur eternal damnation. Finney looked for conversion to produce an intensely emotional episode that essentially altered people's sense of self, resulting in a spiritual rebirth and a deeply transformed sense of their relationship to the world.

of where they stood on the theological continuum, all respected the essential role of repentance.

A SAD CONCLUSION

We discover in this brief bit of church history a point of caution. From the period of the European Reformation to very recently, the main area of contention regarding repentance focused on the question, "Which comes first: God's grace or our repentance?" The problem we face today as a Church is that, as a rule, we've nothing more to say about repentance. We've virtually dropped it from the evangelical vocabulary. Truth be told, it's rare for a theological dispute to even arise in our midst, as our concerns are mainly centered not on proper theology but on proper methodology. While many people have attacked Finney for his theatrical "measures," which they say he used to manipulate people to make a decision for Christ, *at least* he was willing to talk about repentance. In the present day, so many of our churches have maintained the manipulation, but have thrown out the call to repentance.

A Reciprocal Problem

Some may be uncomfortable with phrases such as "godly sorrow," "grief and grieving," "uneasy soul," and "troubled heart" for a different reason. There are many churches that have resisted the evangelical drift toward secularization, treasure classic Protestant theology, and seek to honor Christ in worship. Nevertheless, these churches tend to have a visceral reaction to the above phrases because they mentally associate them with the excesses of "revivalism." But in many of these churches, the pendulum has swung to the opposite extreme so that they, too, have missed the heart of repentance.

Recall the definition of repentance taught by the catechism mentioned above, which reads, "Repentance unto life is a saving grace, whereby a sinner, *out of a true sense of his sin*, and apprehension of the mercy of God in Christ, doth, with grief and hatred of his sin, turn from it unto God, with full purpose of, and endeavor after, *new obedience*" (italics mine). The little phrase "out of a true sense of his sin" implies that God's Spirit has imparted to the sinner a sure idea of the horrid nature of his sin whereby he now feels a deep angst over it before a holy God. It is this sense of sin that results in "new obedience."

While I applaud churches that have continued to remain steadfastly orthodox in the face of the growing encroachment of worldly values in other churches, I still search for empirical evidence of radically changed lives for Christ, that "new obedience" coming from a true sense of sin. The principal area where this evidence is lacking is in these churches' almost universal abandonment of the Great Commission: Christ's charge to get out of our churches and share the gospel with the lost. Conservative, Protestant churches that *ring the bell* before the start of the Sunday morning worship service only to say to their community, "Come and get it," aren't living in new obedience.

Just as in the case of repentance, so also faith involves a dramatic encounter with the Living God.

TRUSTING GOD

What is faith? *Faith is synonymous with trust on Christ alone for the forgiveness of sins.* How are we to understand this trust on Christ? Let me set up this discussion with a look back at some famous artists from the past.

Renaissance art and architecture was consumed with the pursuit of perfection. Artists of the period demonstrated great care for mathematical precision or *absolute form* in their compositions out of a deep and persistent attitude that the intellect can obtain knowledge of God only insofar as physical objects are related to God and reveal Him. Remember, most people didn't have Bibles at that time. There was therefore a much greater emphasis placed upon "natural" theology and the need for the physical world to provide all knowledge of God. To the extent that an artist captured perfection in his work he believed he was helping people capture a vision of the celestial world of God's perfect order. Leonardo da Vinci's famed *Vitruvian man* is a case study in the Renaissance pursuit of the perfect form.

In the end, however, not a single Renaissance man of genius felt he had accomplished perfection in art. Leonardo da Vinci said of his work, "I have offended God and mankind because my work did not reach the quality it should have." Michelangelo was perhaps the greatest painter and sculptor who ever lived. He was so consumed with his pursuit of the perfect form that he was driven nearly mad.

The Reformation

Martin Luther also fell short of perfection, and he knew it. In Luther's case, however, his failure didn't stem from his inability to achieve artistic flawlessness. He failed to live up to the standard of God's holy nature. The burden of Luther's soul magnified as each day he was faced with the gnawing awareness that his religious disciplines as a monk were of no benefit to bringing him into right standing with God. In time, God worked graciously and providentially in Luther's life to bring him to the knowledge of *sola fide*—justification by faith alone.

Now that we have a baseline definition of faith, what else should we know about faith that's vital for the life of the churches?

FAITH UNDER THE MICROSCOPE

First, it's important that we understand the *essence* of saving faith. Hebrews 11:1 defines faith this way, "Now faith is the substance of things hoped for, the evidence of things not seen" (11:1, KJV). In the original Greek, the word translated "substance" is *hupostasis*. Let me explain the meaning of this term by once more looking back into church history for a clue.

In 451, the Council of Calcedon adopted the word "hypostatic" as part of the "Doctrine of the Hypostatic Union" to say that two natures, divine and human, are united in the one person of Christ without mixture or loss of separate identity. Jesus will forever be the God-man, fully God and fully human, two distinct natures in one Person. If you understand that the dual natures of Christ are a hypostatic union, then you might see where I am going in relation to the essence of faith.

The same way that Jesus unites divine and human natures, so also faith is the union of divine and human elements (*hupostasis*). This is how faith can be a "gift" of God (as referenced in Ephesians 2:8) while at the exact same time be something we are responsible to do (as encouraged by such passages as John 3:16).

The Significance of Faith for Our Day

It's important to understand the essence of faith as a divine/human encounter because it challenges the conventional view of faith which, in large part, is responsible for the deterioration of Christianity in the West. Ask the average Christian how they came to faith, and he will likely tell you, "I accepted Jesus." But no one accepts Jesus. Jesus accepts you. God doesn't need our acceptance. But as long as we think that we accept Jesus, the tendency on our parts is to perceive Christianity as a car with us behind the steering wheel and Jesus in the passenger seat. We decide the depth of our service, the nature of our commitment, and the degree to which we will obey His commands, including the Great Commission and the Cultural Mandate. People think and act this way because not once did they take to heart who and what they really are before God, as sinners: vile, putrid, and hell-bound.

But, when we comprehend faith as a divine/human counter, it's obvious that faith wouldn't exist had it not been for the fact that God revealed to us the contemptible nature of our sin before Him and imparted to us the gift of faith. To place trust on Jesus for salvation—having responded to Him as a result of this divine/human encounter—is to understand that Jesus is in the driver's seat and we are His passengers. This person calls Him Lord and seeks to act accordingly in every area of life.

This faith reaction to God's grace in salvation is terribly scarce in a vast array of churches and must be recaptured for revival and reformation to break out.

THE BIBLICAL PICTURE OF FAITH

Now let's turn from the essence of saving faith to what it looks like in action; in other words, its *experiential* side. People whom God has quickened to newness of life respond to Christ in faith according to a specific *profile*. This profile is exampled for us many times in the Bible.

One of the first examples is found in the earliest pages of Genesis, where men began to "call upon the name of the Lord" (Genesis 4:26, see also Romans 10:13, Acts 2:21). When the famine was great in the land, Joseph opened the storehouses to the hungry when "the people cried out" for bread (Genesis 41:55). In the New Testament, we find the publican of Jesus' parable who "was even unwilling to lift up his eyes to heaven, but was beating his breast, saying, 'God, be merciful to me, the sinner'" (Luke 18:13).

Calling upon the name of the Lord. Crying out for bread. Pleading with God for mercy. This is saving faith in the biblical profile. Not a mere intellectual tip of the hat to Christ. Not "Oh yeah, I've accepted Jesus," but a deep urgency, an immediate and forceful resolve to be saved. When's the last time you heard someone "cry out" to God for salvation? Is this what you hear in our churches today? When God revealed to you the contemptible condition of your heart before Him, did you to beat your chest and wail, "God, be merciful to me, the sinner"?

When this is your view of things, you run to Christ, you embrace Christ; indeed, you cry out to Christ to relieve the weight of your sin-sick soul. Read between the lines and imagine the state of mind of those starving during the great famine in Egypt as recorded in Genesis 41. Scores must have been yelling, howling, and shrieking, "Oh, give us bread, lest we die!" Where do you find this kind of Christianity today?

A Day I'll Not Ever Forget

Many years ago, my father took me fishing on Lake Okeechobee in Florida. After catching a few mudfish, which we thought were bass (obviously, neither one of us were experienced fishermen), our boat ran across some underwater grass, which caught the propeller of our engine and popped out the shear pin that keeps the propeller rotating. Suddenly, there we were, wondering why the engine was running but the prop wasn't moving. There was a slight breeze that day on the lake that slowly began to push our little boat back into some tall grass. Slowly, we found ourselves out of the main boating channels, hidden in the "deep weeds." To further an already bad situation, the sun was setting, which meant that unless someone came to our aid soon, we were going to be in big trouble.

Suddenly, my father saw a couple of boats in the far distance heading into the marina, trying to beat the sunset. My father started yelling at the top of his lungs, "Help, help!" Unfortunately, no one heard my father's cries for help and continued to head in. But my dad kept yelling for help. His operatic tenor voice carried like a siren across the waters. Finally, a boat came close enough to us so that the captain was able to hear my father, and he rescued us. What fools we felt like when we arrived safely back at the marina only to discover that there was an entire box of shear-pins in the boat the whole time!

My father's desperate cry for help wasn't merely understandable. It was justifiable. People who know they're facing life-threatening circumstances cry out for help. Those who have seen their souls swing in the balances of God's law, the horrendous penalty of sin, whose lives have literally passed before their eyes, call upon the Name of the Lord for salvation with earnestness, profound and immediate. This is faith.

THE WALK OF FAITH

It's also immeasurably important to know that faith is not a momentary decision, but something God calls us to exercise each day. It should take little to see that those who've encountered the Living God according to the biblical profile of faith will naturally desire to walk by faith. Paul encourages this walk knowing the temptations we face to revert back to a works-based mentality (Galatians 5:16, 21). Our tendency is to accept Jesus by faith, but then quickly return to trusting in our own abilities, intellectual prowess, and grit to deal with the obstacles we face in life. We also resolve to work harder to be better disciples. Isn't it strange how so many of us easily claim no fear of tomorrow, but in the daily push and shove of life, walk with fear? Is there an inconsistency here?

Dear reader, let's all assume our need to walk in the freedom of faith on a daily basis, to confess before God that just as we are totally dependent on His grace for salvation, so also we are totally dependent on His grace for sanctification and for daily living. If we are saved by faith, let us therefore walk by faith.

In those times when you feel tempted to revert back to a works-based lifestyle, be encouraged by this thought: *If God can get you into heaven by grace through faith, He can get you through a day by grace through faith.* You just need to stop *trying* and start *dying.* Die to self each day, and walk by faith.

Biblical repentance and faith automatically engender a conversation about holiness. It's this last part of the gospel message that's also obviously wanting among so many of the churches of today but must be retrieved so that we might again live our utmost for his highest.

12

Where the Rubber Meets the Road

"No attribute of God is more dreadful to sinners than His holiness."

—MATTHEW HENRY

FROM AN OBSERVATIONAL POINT of view, compare the average Christian to the average non-Christian and, generally speaking, what do you see? One goes to church on Sunday, the other might but likely doesn't. One shows some level of interest in Christian theology, the other likely has very little interest at all. One anticipates attending some sort of mid-week, Christian corporate gathering, the other probably doesn't. We could go on, but let me stop to ask a question. Where do you see similarity between the two? In how they live. These days, it's become increasingly difficult to discern any real difference between the way Christians and non-Christians live. It's a question of ethics.

Those who make claim to the holiness of Christ, but show no manifestation of the Holy One who indwells them, are close to Jesus in their profession, but closer still to the atheist in practice. Such people are not fooling the Holy God of heaven. Paul couldn't be more to the point. "They profess to know God, but by their deeds they deny Him, being detestable and disobedient and worthless for any good deed" (Titus 1:16). How can a person whose lifestyle is basically indistinguishable from the heathen world be certain of his salvation? He may confess a new life and that the Spirit of holiness now occupies him like a guard, but if what he professes isn't seen to bear testimony with his outward acts, then how can this man, or any who observe him, have confidence that God has truly separated him unto Himself? What the puritans and Jonathan Edwards called "Experiential Religion" is not to be confused with charismatic affectations of body and soul in worship. Its concern is a passionate desire to be separate from the world and one with God and with godliness.

PURITY AND THE GOOD NEWS

The call to holiness is contained in the gospel. Following the Old Testament prophets, both Jesus and John the Baptist called people to "repent" (Matthew 3:2, Mark 1:15). The repentant soul is one that shows forth a radical change of behavior in thought and action, leading to holy living. The call to holiness was an obligatory part of the message preached by the disciples who Jesus sent out to evangelize the world (Matthew 10, Luke 10). And Paul prays that Christians will be wholly consecrated to God. "Now may the God of peace Himself *sanctify you entirely*; and may your spirit and soul and body be preserved complete, without blame at the coming of our Lord Jesus Christ" (1 Thessalonians 5:23, italics added).

How at ease we are to adjoin God to our lives with little or no change in our behavior. But such is not the claim of the true gospel on us. Holy living necessitates a willingness to walk according to a new, God-centered set of priorities. One way to think about this new set of priorities is according to what Paul calls the "obedience of faith" (Romans 1:5). Paul uses this descriptive phrase out of his concern that the gentile believers at the Church at Rome understand that the faith of Abraham must be linked to obedience to God or else faith is horribly inconsistent with the Lordship of Christ.

Paul would be very disappointed to see the extent to which the gospel's demand of holiness has been marginalized by so many of today's churches. Where is the fear of God in our churches? We have made God common. We find churches quick to talk of God's love, mercy, and grace, but slow to take up the implications of his holiness, including His judgment and wrath. Isn't it funny how the church of today only wants to hear of the attributes of God that a pagan world stresses? Even though people like a comfortable God because He can do nothing *to* you, a comfortable God can also do nothing *for* you. The Psalmist counters this pretentious view of God. "Who will not fear, O Lord, and glorify Your name? For You alone are holy" (Revelation 15:4a).

How Far We Have Fallen

In his commentary on Isaiah 6:3, John Calvin observes of the Seraphim who surround the Throne of God, "The angels never cease from their melody in singing the praises of God, as the holiness of God supplies us with inexhaustible reasons for them."[1] Calvin says that not only does God's holiness inspire the angels to worship God, but also, as a result of His great holiness, we too have "inexhaustible reasons" to sing His praises. Moreover, in sheer distinction to the abuses of the Roman Catholicism of their day, God's holiness motivated all of the Reformers to do and to teach all things *soli Deo gloria* (to the glory of God alone).

Today we live in a state of affairs reminiscent of that which the Reformers faced on the eve of the Reformation. The holiness of God is hidden from sight, and consequently, our doctrine is sloppy, our ethics are generally indistinguishable from the world, our worship is chummy, our claim to His blessings is hasty, our view of the condition of our souls is incautious, our attitude toward the lost is passive, and our response to change is dismissive, bordering on callous.

In our disrespect for God's holiness, we market the name of Jesus like IZOD. "Got Jesus" bumper stickers symbolize our best effort at reaching a fallen world with the Name that is above all names. But by reducing the holy name of God to a marketing device, we play marbles with the diamonds of God. God is not common, ordinary, or casual. God is not your "good buddy." He's not the "man upstairs." And you and Jesus don't have your "own thing going." He is God. God is holy. He's to be worshipped and glorified in every area of life.

THE ROOT OF THE PROBLEM

As I've already mentioned in my comments on repentance in the previous chapter, a thirst for holiness is lacking from the lives of many professed believers today, in large part because they work from a wrong view of conversion. In hindsight, most Christians remember themselves as animated, bustling human beings who, yes, had sinned against God and were in need of His forgiveness, but who never internalized the aggregate decadence of their hearts and their need to walk in holiness before Him.

---

1. John Calvin, *Commentary on the Book of Prophet Isaiah*. See biblestudy.churches .net/CCEL/C/CALVIN/COMMENTA/WORK/ISAIAH/ISA101.RTF

In contrast, total depravity means the heart of the unbeliever is deader than a doornail. Although fallen man puts his pants on in the morning like everyone else, spiritually speaking, he's not vibrantly alive, but graveyard dead. It's God's Holy Spirit who raises sinners to newness of life. This is what it means to be "born again." (John 3:3). And He's not called the "Holy" Spirit for nothing. The Spirit of life that now indwells you is set on transforming every part of you in compliance with the Holy nature of God.

The Failure of Contemporary Evangelism

To a large degree, our outreach programs are also to be blamed for the dearth of holiness in our churches. We highlight the need for people to receive Jesus for the gift of eternal life, but we leave quite a bit to be desired when it comes to including the requirement of holiness. The proclamation of the Good News to the lost is subsumed under the higher priority of making "disciples" of all the nations (Matthew 28:18–20). But unless we are producing students of the Master who are set on following Him in holiness, we aren't evangelizing according to the biblical model.

HOLINESS

What is holiness? God's holiness means two things: one positive, the other negative. The positive aspect of His holiness stresses that He is *morally pure*. Moral purity doesn't mean good, but perfect. God is absolutely, unequivocally, morally perfect. God is called the "Holy One of Israel" nearly thirty times in Isaiah and is so called throughout the Old Testament. In the New Testament Jesus is the "Holy One" (1 John 2:20). The name of the third person of the Trinity is the Holy Spirit. The essential nature of God is impeccably untainted, unsullied, and nothing short of spotless.

The negative connotation of Divine holiness means that God is *morally separate* from all that is morally imperfect. God cannot, nor will not, tolerate sin. Not even one. How many times did Adam and Eve sin before God cast them out of the Garden? Once. God has zero tolerance for anyone who falls short of His holiness.

His Holiness Is Far Above All

People counter, "Oh, don't make God out to be too holy because He won't communicate to people." But to bring God down on any level, other than the one He's presently on, you make for yourself an idol. According to classic, Protestant theology, God's holiness is associated with His transcendence. Imagine God's holiness. The fact is that you really can't. The holiness of God transcends even your idea of His holiness. It also transcends any aspect of holiness we possess. The Bible says, "Be ye Holy; for I am Holy" (1 Peter 1:16, KJV). Still, our holiness is only ever a finite image of the perfect holiness of God, which is limitless. God's holiness transcends any thought or experience you may have of his perfect holiness. In fact, *his holiness transcends even the thought you have that His holiness transcends the thought you have of His holiness.* God's transcendence has no mate, no jogging partner, or golf buddy. Nothing goes higher than the transcendent holiness of God and nothing is as holy as the Lord.

Oh, that our worship, doctrine, ethics, and evangelism should once more reflect the awesome holiness of our God!

Making Your Election Sure

God's call to holiness is also a goal of election. Paul writes, "Just as He chose us in Him before the foundation of the world, that we would be holy and blameless before Him in love" (Ephesians 1:4, see also 2 Peter 1:10–11). Have you noticed that Reformed churches stress God's electing grace in salvation while Arminian churches stress holiness? But according to Ephesians 1:4, election and holiness are inseparable. "He chose us in Him . . . that we would be holy and blameless before Him." God elects people to salvation *so that* they will be holy. The church of today suffers terribly from "cheap grace" because so many people don't understand the goal of election: that Christians are to be pure, holy, and undefiled. Hence, many of us ignore the law of God and the requirement of holiness.

Closely related to holiness is the doctrine of sanctification. It's therefore important that we engage in a brief discussion of its nature and import.

SANCTIFICATION

What is sanctification? In those whom God has regenerated, the dominion of sin is destroyed and a new heart and a new Spirit are created. This
new spirit is also called the "new man," or better yet, Christ Himself.
Christ lives in believers through the indwelling presence of the Holy
Spirit. His goal from this point is to weaken in us the taste for the things
of the world, the lusts of the flesh, and to build and strengthen in us new
desires that glorify God.

Sanctification, therefore, isn't to be considered a human work.
We're saved by grace alone through faith on Christ alone. Likewise, we're
sanctified, or cleansed of the remaining stain of sin in our lives, by grace
alone through faith on Christ alone. Sanctification is a grace God works
in us. Certainly, the call to live sanctified lives requires effort on our part.
Nonetheless, this effort ought to be viewed as a *different kind of doing*.
Daily repentance is synonymous with becoming more and more *undone*
before God. It is by confessing our *inability* to live the Christian life,
while drawing upon His grace, presence, and power for holiness, that He
sovereignly makes us more like Him.

The Import of Sanctification

In Ephesians, Paul encourages husbands to love their wives, just as Christ
loved the Church and gave Himself up for her (5:22–25). He then presses
the analogy to teach us why Christ gave His body at the cross for His
Church. It's "so that He might sanctify her" (v. 26). Jesus didn't die just
so people can have "fire insurance." He intends to thoroughly cleanse us
from the stain of sin. He aims to present to Himself a bride without spot or
wrinkle (v. 27). The disingenuous Christian is the picture of the bride who
is determined to meet her groom at the altar without having taken a bath
in a year. But no one shall see God who has not gone through the hard
process of sanctification resulting in true holiness (Hebrews 12:14).

Growth Equal in All Its Parts

In sanctifying us, God does not cleanse parts of our hearts in consecu-
tive order. He cleanses every part of us simultaneously, through the
whole person. God doesn't work on our impatience, then when He has
finished, move to our problem with anger, then to our overindulgences.
He grows us in the image of Christ concurrently. Consider how a baby

grows. Its arm does not shoot out, followed by a leg, followed by the head enlarging. No, the whole baby grows evenly at once. The reader may not be conscious of this fact. You may feel as though anger yet occupies a higher, stronger place of residence in your heart as compared to coveting. But what baby is more aware of the growth of their toes than their brain? This doesn't mean the baby's brain is behind the growth curve.

Slow But Constant Growth

Some people wonder why they don't act more like Christ soon after their conversion. Perhaps this simple analogy will help. Imagine two trees. The first tree is full grown. It represents the old, sinful nature. When Christ enters the life of a sinner, He immediately cuts the roots of the great tree that provide it life. Let's call this "destroying the dominion of sin" (Romans 6:14). Now from the outside the giant tree looks perfectly fine; its fruit still hangs from the branches. But its root is cut, so it's only a matter of time before the tree and its fruit perish completely. This is why the sins that control unbelievers *appear* to prolong for a period. But fear not. With no life support, sin has lost its power over your life and is destined to wither away.

The second is a small tree. It represents the new nature, which is Christ in you. This little tree has roots that are firmly planted in the soil and provide life to the tree. Though outwardly it pales in comparison to the giant tree, it has a future. So, as the giant tree slowly dies off, the little tree slowly grows to maturity, overtaking the giant tree. The end result of this entire process is the perfecting of holiness in the inner man.

SANCTIFICATION AND HOLINESS DISTINGUISHED

There is a fine line to draw between sanctification and holiness. Sanctification is a work of God in us. Holiness is the outward result. Sanctification is a process whereby God transforms our inner man in character to comport with that of His own. Holiness is the felt presence of the new character among people and before God. In sanctification God redirects our priorities. Holiness is the new set of priorities on display.

Time for Reflection

What are your priorities? Consider God's ultimate goal for you, which is to make you like Jesus, against the backdrop of the priorities of the age. Think of the time and energy so many people spend on achieving earthly goals. Indeed, how many Christians are consumed with achieving success in their chosen profession? Perhaps you are one. This person spends countless hours in hard work hoping to become someone of significance and to have a great effect in the world. But what happens when, after years of trying and praying, success fails to materialize? This is when hearts begin to fret, fretting begets failed expectations, failed expectations beget a sense of hopelessness, and hopelessness begets the death of a vision.

Do you worry yourself sick over trying to be the next Bill Gates? Are you a preacher who is ruining himself trying to be the next Billy Graham? It's a tragic state because what is of ultimate importance to God is not that you make it to the *top of the heap*, but that you are conformed to the express image of His Son. God will permit failures to occur in your life, even the death of a vision, if He believes that such failures will enhance your sanctification. Do you fully understand that, although God is concerned with your earthly success, He is more concerned with conforming you to Jesus?

THE SURRENDERED LIFE

Another way to think in terms of the Gospel's call to holy living is according to a little phrase—*total surrender*. In years past, it was typical for preachers to call people to entire submissiveness to Jesus. In fact, going all the way back to the early nineteenth century, we find this idea taking a central place in an important revival. The year was 1818. The evangelist was Asahel Nettleton. He came to the Congregational Church in Eastford, Connecticut in the month of December. The fact that Nettleton had been invited is itself rather amazing for the church had called to its pulpit a Universalist pastor just four years earlier. The evangelist arrived to find only twenty members, six of whom were elderly men.

It took only a brief time for Nettleton to see that the people of the church had become careless about their souls before a holy God. Nettleton's clear and forceful preaching emphasized the dangers of sin, the immediacy of God's wrath, and the free gift of God's sovereign grace in Christ. His listeners, now feeling the crushing weight of their sins, and being deeply troubled in heart and mind over their depravity and wretchedness, heard Nettleton call them to unconditional submission to the grace of God in Christ Jesus. Revival broke out. By the following June, fifty-eight people had become Christians and members of the church, not a small number for a rural, Connecticut church in those early years.

The Current Debate

Many individuals are uncomfortable with the phrase "total surrender" or "total submission." Some contend that it promotes total sanctification this side of heaven, while others believe it places too much focus on human responsibility and not enough on God's sovereignty in the process of sanctification. But, more than not, the reason it has disappeared from the evangelical vocabulary is because the average congregant simply doesn't want to be totally surrendered to Christ. Because evangelicalism is the picture of the tail wagging the dog, pastors avoid mention of total surrender because it "sends the wrong message."

But the Bible is full of stories and direct commands that stimulate us to think about being totally surrendered to Christ. It's the picture of Isaac, beaten by God at the bottom of the ravine, crying out, "I will not let you go until you bless me" (Genesis 32:26). It's that of Mary taking a pound of very costly perfume of pure nard and anointing the feet of Jesus, and wiping His feet with her hair (John 12:1–11). These biblical directives are merely another way to say, "You shall be holy, for I am holy" (1 Peter 1:16).

Uplifted Hands

Total surrender to Christ is very important in the context of spiritual warfare. As long as Moses held both of his arms in the air, the Israelites prevailed against the evil Amalekites. But as soon as he dropped his hands, Amalek prevailed. Aaron and Hur, seeing the obvious, took a stone and put it under him, and they each supported his hands, one on one side and one on the other. This lasted until sunset with the result that Amalek and his people were defeated (Exodus 17:8–16).

How does this story illustrate the relationship of total surrender and success in spiritual warfare? If a man stuck a gun in your back to rob you of your money, what would he likely command you to do? He'd say, "Stick 'em up!" *Hands in the air are the universal sign of submission.* To place your hands high in the air is to say to God, "I surrender." Now my point is not to encourage the lifting of hands during a worship service, though I'm not against this practice. The more important point to draw from this lesson is that Moses' uplifted hands are a vivid picture of total surrender to God and that with his surrender came a great victory over the enemies of God. What a marvelous truth we find in this biblical example. When our hearts are surrendered to Him, victories on the field of battle are not far behind.

Wearing Christ

The surrendered Christian is one who views himself as a *suit of clothes* for Christ. Imagine a man's suit. What fills it and holds it up? The person inhabiting the suit. Likewise, the only thing that fills and sustains the Christian each second is the life-occupying presence of Christ. Paul reflects this thought when he says of himself, "I have been crucified with Christ and I no longer live, but Christ lives in me; and the life which I now live in the flesh I live by faith in the Son of God, who loved me and gave himself for me" (Galatians 2:20).

Now imagine this ridiculous scenario: a man walking one direction and his clothes walking in another. This is how we look to God when we attempt to walk in the flesh apart from the Holy Spirit of Christ, who occupies us and gives us life. To be born again means that we are no longer our own, but have been raised to newness of life and now belong to God. He is our life. To daily think of oneself as a suit of clothes for Jesus stimulates one to be totally submitted to Christ without the chore of legalism.

Favorable to God

Still another way to think of total submission to Christ is according to what it means to be a *God-pleaser*. The Bible says that "Those who are in the flesh cannot please God" (Romans 8:8). When we think of what it means to please someone, we naturally think of making someone happy in a modest way. For instance, someone might say, "I filed the papers and pleased my boss." Or, "I pleased my mother by taking out the garbage." But in the Bible the word "please" carries far greater import. To be a God-pleaser is the highest honor that can be paid to a Christian. At the end of 365 years, Enoch was translated without seeing death. Why? He had pleased God (Hebrews 11:5). We please God when we walk with Him in a spirit of total surrender.

Are you being led by the Spirit? Do you consider yourself a suit of clothes for Christ? Are you anxious over the patterns of sin in your life? Do you desire to be a God-pleaser?

A Final Word...

Much that is wrong with our churches has been observed in this book, but not to the exclusion of what is right with God, and what can again be right with us, should we pant for Him as the deer pants for the water brook. Like most of the brooks in and around ancient Israel that were surrounded by hard terrain, we have traveled through and over quite a few rough spots in our church-life together to get to some answers. Certainly not everything is wrong with us, nor should the very idea of "new" be considered an abomination. As I said with respect to what goes on in a worship service, for example, I am willing to embrace much that is new, especially new forms of expressive singing. We don't live in the first or the sixteenth centuries anymore.

What does need a good look, however, includes the state of preaching and teaching in our pulpits, the stress on innovation in ministry over biblical method, the lack of properly prescribed church discipline in many churches, the unwillingness of people to use their spiritual gifts for Jesus, and more. Unfortunately, there are other areas we could talk about not mentioned in this volume. We also covered briefly the main rationales for these deficiencies: that in their effort to reach a so-called postmodern audience, many of our evangelical churches have themselves become bastions of postmodernism, and also the sheer apathy of too many Christians toward radical living for Christ, which is the mark of "Laodicea."

But, as I also confidently stated, the fresh winds of reformation are in the air. Look to the heavens, those of you who care, for He incites Himself to vindicate His holy Name among the nations as He did in the past. He kindles in His hand the impending fire of awakening, resulting in revival, that it would touch our nation, your nation, my church, your church, my family, your family—all that we are, and all that we should ever hope to be.